D0201084

FIVE CITIES OF REFUGE

FIVE CITIES OF REFUGE

WEEKLY REFLECTIONS ON
GENESIS,
EXODUS,
LEVITICUS,
NUMBERS,
AND DEUTERONOMY

LAWRENCE KUSHNER
AND DAVID MAMET

SCHOCKEN BOOKS ■ NEW YORK

Copyright © 2003 by Rabbi Lawrence Kushner and David Mamet

All rights reserved under International and Pan-American Copyright
Conventions. Published in the United States by Schocken Books, a
division of Random House, Inc., New York, and simultaneously in
Canada by Random House of Canada Limited, Toronto. Distributed
by Pantheon Books, a division of Random House, Inc., New York.

Schocken and colophon are registered trademarks of
Random House, Inc.

Library of Congress Cataloging-in-Publication Data
Kushner, Lawrence, 1943–
Five cities of refuge : weekly reflections on Genesis, Exodus, Leviticus,
Numbers, and Deuteronomy / Lawrence Kushner and David Mamet.
p. cm.
ISBN 0-8052-4220-1
1. Bible. O.T. Pentateuch—Meditations. I. Mamet, David. II. Title.

BS1225.54.K87 2003
222'.106—dc21   2003042790

www.schocken.com

Book design by Iris Weinstein

Printed in the United States of America

First Edition
2 4 6 8 9 7 5 3 1

CONTENTS

INTRODUCTION

We have studied the weekly lection together now for several years. Our *hevruta* (learning partnership) originally began with an introductory course on the Hebrew of the Hebrew Bible which Kushner taught at a synagogue in Sudbury, Massachusetts, and where Mamet was a member. Each of those classes, like this book, was based on a few key verses from the weekly biblical portion which were central to one of its principal themes. When the course was done, we decided to continue sharing our reactions to the biblical text over a weekly breakfast at Johnny's Delicatessen in Newton Centre, Massachusetts.

Our premise was that the biblical text always knew more than we did. A passage you suspect may be in error, mistaken, corrupt, incomplete or just plain wrong, offers only two real options: Either it's stupid or you are. If you choose the former, as many moderns do, you effectively cut yourself off from anything you don't agree with or understand. You place your-self above the text and can no longer be instructed or chastened by it. But, if you will venture the tradi-tional temerity to choose the latter, then every book, every verse, every letter—especially the ones you don't agree with or understand—become a potential source of new wisdom and growth. We have tried to approach scripture with some of this reverence.

This, of course, only raises the obvious problem of literalism. Jewish fundamentalism, it seems to us, dif-fers from other literalist traditions in one important way. Others claim that because the biblical text is a vessel for God's word, it must be taken literally. Jews go further. If God is somehow *in* the biblical text, then not only must we revere the literal meaning of each word, we must assume that each word has *infinite* meaning. And that means that arguments are in-escapable. Surely anything less would only trivialize sacred words.

Imagine, for instance, that you are a therapist. To your trained ear, anything said by your patient has many potential nuanced shades, associations, and levels of possible interpretation. Now imagine that your patient is God. Surely the words of the Source of All Words must be infinitely meaningful. In the language of the Zohar, the master text of Jewish mys-ticism, "The stories in the bible couldn't be about what they seem to be about, otherwise we could write better stories!" The holiness of sacred text, in other words, comes precisely from its ability to continuously generate new interpretations.

Surely one of the strangest institutions of the Hebrew Bible is a little-known divine instruction to Moses and the Israelites that, after they cross the Jordan River, they are to designate cities to which someone who has committed accidental manslaughter might flee from those seeking vengeance for blood guilt. According to the Book of Numbers, there were to be six of these *aray miklat*, cities of refuge. The Pentateuch, of course, has only five volumes: Genesis, Exodus, Leviticus, Numbers, and Deuteronomy; if you will, *five* cities of refuge where those of us who have committed accidental (or purposeful) transgressions might turn for solace and safety. Indeed, they have been a destination and refuge for centuries of students and teachers of the Bible. The Five Books of Moses are cities of solace and safety. In the following pages, we respectfully offer the record of our own weekly visits. And we hope that ours will inspire yours.

In the week when we read: *"A person cannot see and live."*
5763

> L.K.
> *San Francisco*
> D.M.
> *Santa Monica*

FIVE CITIES OF REFUGE

וַיְכֻלּוּ הַשָּׁמַיִם וְהָאָרֶץ וְכָל־צְבָאָם: וַיְכַל אֱלֹקִים בַּיּוֹם הַשְּׁבִיעִי מְלַאכְתּוֹ אֲשֶׁר עָשָׂה וַיִּשְׁבֹּת בַּיּוֹם הַשְּׁבִיעִי מִכָּל־מְלַאכְתּוֹ אֲשֶׁר עָשָׂה: וַיְבָרֶךְ אֱלֹקִים אֶת־יוֹם הַשְּׁבִיעִי וַיְקַדֵּשׁ אֹתוֹ כִּי בוֹ שָׁבַת מִכָּל־מְלַאכְתּוֹ אֲשֶׁר־בָּרָא אֱלֹקִים לַעֲשׂוֹת:

And the heavens and the earth and all their hosts were finished. And on the seventh day God finished the work that God had been doing, and God rested on the seventh day from all the work that God had done. And God blessed the seventh day and sanctified it because on it God rested from all the work of creation that God had done.

LK

The four-letter Name of God—*yod, hey, vav,* and *hey*—is God's most intimate Name. Made from the root letters of the Hebrew verb "to be," originally it probably meant something like the "One who brings into being all that is." It is the ultimate Name of being's holiness, the one we must never waste (or, "take in vain"). Jewish mystical tradition explains that what is wrong with our present world must therefore be traceable to a corresponding defect in the Name itself: The letters are broken apart from one another. Something on high is fractured. And the ultimate task of humanity is, through right action and right intention, to bring them together again. Such meditations are called *yihudim,* unifications.

The *"vaYechulu* (And they were finished)," as the above three verses from Genesis are called, is traditionally chanted as a poetic introduction to the *kiddush,* or Sanctification prayer, prior to the Sabbath meal. The world-work is done; let us now join God by sanctifying the seventh day. We bless God's work—and our own—by quitting. The work *and* the rest, together make the world. They are inseparable. (Or at least, if they were, the world-work would truly be complete, redemption at last.)

The chapters in our present Bible are not of Jewish origin. They inadvertently separate the six days of creation of Genesis, Chapter 1, from the *"vaYechulu* (And they were finished),"* of the seventh day in Genesis, Chapter 2. But perhaps that's the way it really is: Our work and our rest are severed, split apart. All too often, they bear little or no relationship to one another. Our world is broken. This, in turn, may explain the cryptic old tradition that appends to the beginning of *"vaYechulu* (And they were finished)"* the last few words of the preceding chapter, ". . . and there was evening and there was morning, a sixth day." The Hebrew for "the sixth day" is *yom haShishi.* The first letter respectively of each word is *yod* and *hey,* which, when joined with the first letter respectively of "And they [the heavens and the earth] were finished . . ." is *vav* and *hey,* together spelling *yod, hey, vav,* and *hey,* the ineffable Name, the Name of the One who brings into being all that is, the Name of God. At last the sweat and the sigh inseparable.

DM

"Closure" is a concept foreign to Jewish tradition. It is an overwhelmingly secular, modern, and arrogant idea—that one, by an act of will, manipulation, or aggression can "complete" a disturbing experience.

This mythical mechanical completion means triumph over: fate, chance, anger, grief, or injustice, and is achievable only through oblivion or repression.

The struggle to deal with an unjust, confusing, incomprehensible world does not impede our life; it *is* our life.

Bereshit, the very beginning of the Torah, counsels that there is and will be no completion, there is no "closure," and that this lack is not to be decried but, in fact, celebrated.

GENESIS / *BERESHIT*

2. GENESIS 6:9–13 / NOAH

אֵלֶּה תּוֹלְדֹת נֹחַ נֹחַ אִישׁ צַדִּיק תָּמִים הָיָה
בְּדֹרֹתָיו אֶת־הָאֱלֹקִים הִתְהַלֶּךְ־נֹחַ: וַיּוֹלֶד נֹחַ שְׁלֹשָׁה
בָנִים אֶת־שֵׁם אֶת־חָם וְאֶת־יָפֶת: וַתִּשָּׁחֵת הָאָרֶץ לִפְנֵי
הָאֱלֹקִים וַתִּמָּלֵא הָאָרֶץ חָמָס: וַיַּרְא אֱלֹקִים
אֶת־הָאָרֶץ וְהִנֵּה נִשְׁחָתָה כִּי־הִשְׁחִית כָּל־בָּשָׂר
אֶת־דַּרְכּוֹ עַל־הָאָרֶץ: וַיֹּאמֶר אֱלֹקִים לְנֹחַ קֵץ כָּל־בָּשָׂר
בָּא לְפָנַי כִּי־מָלְאָה הָאָרֶץ חָמָס מִפְּנֵיהֶם וְהִנְנִי
מַשְׁחִיתָם אֶת־הָאָרֶץ:

This is the family line of Noah. Noah was a righteous man, blameless in his generation. Noah walked with God. Noah fathered three sons: Shem, Ham, and Japhet. Now the earth had become defiled before God so that it was filled with violence. And God looked at the earth and, behold, all humanity had defiled its way on the land. So God said to Noah, "I have decided to destroy humanity because the earth is filled with violence because of it: Behold, now I will destroy them with the earth."

Rabbinic tradition is conflicted over what to do with Noah. On the one hand, the biblical text describes him as a *tzaddik*, a righteous man who walked with God. On the other, unlike Abraham and Moses, Noah never protested God's harsh decree—not so much as even one peep. How righteous could a man be who watched the destruction of an entire generation in silence?

Hasidic tradition disdainfully calls Noah a *tzaddik im pelz*, a righteous man in a fur coat, who, instead of helping others build a fire to warm themselves, just pulls his own coat tighter around himself. When push comes to shove, he only looks out for himself. Indeed, Rabbi Aaron Samuel Tameret has suggested that to stand aboard that ark and witness the end of humanity was Noah's ultimate punishment.

Levi Yitzhak of Berditchev offers a solution based on an insight into the personality of a religious leader. The difference between the two kinds of *tzaddikim* does not derive from the presence or absence of some special moral fiber. It's not even the result of the instinct for self-preservation. What enables a true *tzaddik* to rise in the defense of the world—even when that world is uniformly and unrepentantly evil—is an expression of one's own self-worth. Noah, suggests the Berditchever, said to himself, "Who am I to be worthy to challenge God's decree?" And so he did nothing. His failure was his humility. And, even though it is the source of all human wickedness (and would doubtless make Levi Yitzhak cringe), every real *tzaddik,* sooner or later, needs a little bit of arrogance. A righteous man must believe in the power of his own righteousness.

DM

Tolstoy wrote that there has never been an intelligent man who, looking around him, did not say, "Surely the corruption of the world is such that it must be obliterated soon."

His observation suggests the existence of two human traits: a sense of social order (if present only in outrage at its absence), and a sense of cosmic order—or, say, of the existence of God.

But how can one reconcile these two seemingly opposed human perceptions?

Perhaps they coalesce in the human capacity to ask that very question, which is to say, in the study of Torah.

3. GENESIS 12:1–3 / LEKH-LEKHA

וַיֹּאמֶר יְדֹוָד אֶל־אַבְרָם לֶךְ־לְךָ מֵאַרְצְךָ וּמִמּוֹלַדְתְּךָ
וּמִבֵּית אָבִיךָ אֶל־הָאָרֶץ אֲשֶׁר אַרְאֶךָּ: וְאֶעֶשְׂךָ לְגוֹי
גָּדוֹל וַאֲבָרֶכְךָ וַאֲגַדְּלָה שְׁמֶךָ וֶהְיֵה בְּרָכָה: וַאֲבָרֲכָה
מְבָרֲכֶיךָ וּמְקַלֶּלְךָ אָאֹר וְנִבְרְכוּ בְךָ כֹּל מִשְׁפְּחֹת
הָאֲדָמָה:

And the Lord said to Avram: "Leave your land, your birthplace, and your parent's home for the land that I will show you. And I will make of you a great nation and I will bless you and I will make your name great and you will be a blessing. And I will bless those who bless you and curse those who curse you, and all the families of the earth shall be blessed through you."

The text could have just said, "And Avram set out," or, "God told Avram to go forth." That would have been mythically elegant. But instead, God gets personal. The first thing God says to the first Jew is "leave your *parents'* home." And as the ancient rabbinic dictum has it: What happens to the parents is already a sign of what will happen to the children.

The great, unending psychospiritual task of every human being is separating from his or her parents. Loved or hated, near or far, living or long dead, it's never done. We spend our days trying to be who we imagine we want to be and *not* who *they* wanted us to be. We strive with all our cunning to infuriate them even as we secretly yearn to make them smile and to fulfill their secret dreams. But before we can finish, or even figure out what's going on, we have our own children and the whole thing starts all over again from the other side.

In any case, the text is clear: Doing business with this new, imageless, and as yet unnamed God means to leave home, to commence the struggle, to believe unto your dying breath that you will break free from their orbit. But as you grow older—much older—you would be grateful if you could just (even occasionally) strike a balance between your parents and yourself and between yourself and your children. Maybe that is the land that God will show us *and* what it means to be a blessing.

DM

There is a communal pathogen called anti-Semitism. It is a delusion, the hallmark of which is, to the deluded, its aura of *revealed truth*.

In a world overcome by this insanity, "the Jew" is reviled for his most immediately apparent attribute—the poor Jew for his poverty, the rich Jew for his riches; the immigrant for his impertinence, the long-established for his intransigence.

We see the patriot Jew taxed with his efforts to "pass," and the sequestered with his "clannishness." The Jew in the Diaspora is an outsider, and the United Nations brands Zionism a race crime.

What is the cause of the sickness, of the mental plague of anti-Semitism? Perhaps the commandment, in *Lekh-lekha*, to *stand apart*.

And, *indeed*, most Jews feel that, as the Torah states, those societies which bless us will be blessed—for, what does the Jew do while he stands apart? *He considers*.

וַיְהִי אַחַר הַדְּבָרִים הָאֵלֶּה וְהָאֱלֹקִים נִסָּה אֶת־אַבְרָהָם
וַיֹּאמֶר אֵלָיו אַבְרָהָם וַיֹּאמֶר הִנֵּנִי: וַיֹּאמֶר קַח־נָא
אֶת־בִּנְךָ אֶת־יְחִידְךָ אֲשֶׁר־אָהַבְתָּ אֶת־יִצְחָק וְלֶךְ־לְךָ
אֶל־אֶרֶץ הַמֹּרִיָּה וְהַעֲלֵהוּ שָׁם לְעֹלָה עַל אַחַד הֶהָרִים
אֲשֶׁר אֹמַר אֵלֶיךָ: וַיַּשְׁכֵּם אַבְרָהָם בַּבֹּקֶר וַיַּחֲבֹשׁ
אֶת־חֲמֹרוֹ וַיִּקַּח אֶת־שְׁנֵי נְעָרָיו אִתּוֹ וְאֵת יִצְחָק בְּנוֹ
וַיְבַקַּע עֲצֵי עֹלָה וַיָּקָם וַיֵּלֶךְ אֶל־הַמָּקוֹם אֲשֶׁר־אָמַר־לוֹ
הָאֱלֹקִים: בַּיּוֹם הַשְּׁלִישִׁי וַיִּשָּׂא אַבְרָהָם אֶת־עֵינָיו
וַיַּרְא אֶת־הַמָּקוֹם מֵרָחֹק:

A
nd it came to pass after these things that God
tested Abraham and said to him, "Abraham."
And he said, "I am ready." And He said, "Take
your son, your only one, whom you love, Isaac, and go
forth to the Land of Moriah and sacrifice him there on one
of the mountains I will designate." So Abraham got up
early in the morning, saddled his ass, and took two of his
servants with him and Isaac his son. And he split the wood
for the sacrifice. Then he arose and went to the place that
God had said. And on the third day, Abraham raised his
eyes and, off in the distance, he saw the place.

According to the Midrash, this was the last of ten trials by which God tested Abraham. The first began with the same conspicuous Hebrew phrase, *"Lekh-lekha,* Go forth [for yourself]," when God told Abraham to leave his own father's house. The story thus ends the way it began: *"Lekh-lekha,* Go forth [for yourself]." The boy is father to the man. It's so primal, it's the touchstone for all religious learning. Why else would the rabbis have us read, of all things, such an awe-full story on Rosh Hashanah? The parents whisper to their progeny, "You know, I almost killed you once." "Happy New Year, Daddy." "Sit up straight."

On two separate occasions, the text says of Abraham and Isaac, "And they went, both of them together." But after whatever it was that happened up there on that peak, we read only, "And Abraham returned to his servants." Isaac, we must assume, went down the other side, alone.

The name of the mountain, Moriah, means "awe-full." Tradition claims it will become the site of the Temple, the center of the world. Sinai, where the Torah was given, is ownerless and unknown. The holiest place known to Jews is the scene of a near sacrifice. The Temple is built where the older generation almost kills the younger but forbears at the last possible moment. Only a three-day's journey from home.

If you raise your eyes, you can see it off in the distance.

DM

And God tested Abraham. He said to him, "Abraham," and Abraham answered, "Here I am."

Having acknowledged the voice of God, Abraham commits himself to do God's will.

The true act of acceptance, however, the inception of the Jewish religion, is not Abraham's willingness to sacrifice his beloved son, but his willingness to accept the command *not* to do so.

Judaism repudiates what would, it seems, be the most ancient and prevalent form of propitiation of the gods: infant sacrifice. Donation to the gods of that which, beyond question, was the most precious possession of the donor, must have been the ultimate primordial attempt at eradication of anxiety: "How can the gods not accept this greatest of gifts—they *must.*"

We see the survival memory of child-sacrifice inverted in the Santa Claus myth, where a representative of the sun god sneaks into the house at the winter solstice. Again, inverting cause and effect, the messenger takes away a child in his sack; it is the gods who are propitiated, not the child. Recall the rhetoric of the Vietnam War, in which sixty thousand young men were sacrificed to defend "our position in the world"—they were the unfortunate infants, sent as an offering to the unfathomable Powers.

We hear the rhetoric in the speech of parents who, doubting the true educational abilities of their school, send the children in any case to be "socialized."

Abraham was acting as part of a known, and accepted, primeval and still extant tradition.

As he stands ready to sacrifice his son, a messenger of God speaks. The messenger calls, "Abraham, Abraham," repeating his name twice, as the command to cease is harder to accept even than the original command to kill. And Abraham obeys; he accepts the word of God's Messenger and stays his hand, even though such restraint visits upon him, and upon the Jewish race, the various burdens of uncertainty.

וַיֵּצֵא יִצְחָק לָשׂוּחַ בַּשָּׂדֶה לִפְנוֹת עָרֶב וַיִּשָּׂא עֵינָיו
וַיַּרְא וְהִנֵּה גְמַלִּים בָּאִים: וַתִּשָּׂא רִבְקָה אֶת־עֵינֶיהָ
וַתֵּרֶא אֶת־יִצְחָק וַתִּפֹּל מֵעַל הַגָּמָל: וַתֹּאמֶר אֶל־הָעֶבֶד
מִי־הָאִישׁ הַלָּזֶה הַהֹלֵךְ בַּשָּׂדֶה לִקְרָאתֵנוּ וַיֹּאמֶר הָעֶבֶד
הוּא אֲדֹנִי וַתִּקַּח הַצָּעִיף וַתִּתְכָּס: וַיְסַפֵּר הָעֶבֶד לְיִצְחָק
אֵת כָּל־הַדְּבָרִים אֲשֶׁר עָשָׂה: וַיְבִאֶהָ יִצְחָק הָאֹהֱלָה
שָׂרָה אִמּוֹ וַיִּקַּח אֶת־רִבְקָה וַתְּהִי־לוֹ לְאִשָּׁה וַיֶּאֱהָבֶהָ
וַיִּנָּחֵם יִצְחָק אַחֲרֵי אִמּוֹ:

And Isaac went out into the field to meditate in the evening. And he raised his eyes and he saw and behold, camels were approaching. And Rebecca raised her eyes, and when she saw Isaac, she jumped down from the camel. And she said to the servant, "Who is this man in the field coming to meet us?" And the servant said, "He is my master." She took the veil and covered herself. And the servant told Isaac of everything he had done. And Isaac brought her into the tent of Sarah his mother. And he took Rebecca and she became his wife, and he loved her and Isaac was comforted after the death of his mother.

Everyone, it seems, is looking off into the distance, trying to get a leg up on the future, hoping for clairvoyance. It's the most natural thing in the world; we all do it. Successful people seem to have a knack for intuiting the future and then being there a few minutes before everyone else. But even though Abraham "raises his eyes" and sees in the distance the place where he believes he will slaughter his son, he does not yet know it's "only a test." Isaac too "raises his eyes" and sees camels coming, but he does not yet know they are bringing the woman he will marry. Even Rebecca, on the caravan, "raises her eyes" and sees a man coming toward her, but she does not yet know it is Isaac. They all see things in the distance, but there's always more in the distance than we can discern. Something *else* is coming down. We only realize this in retrospect.

DM

My teacher, Rabbi Kushner, would stand on the *bimah* and extemporize his translation of the week's *parasha*. His English was colloquial, and magnificent. Later, I had the great good fortune to be taught by Rabbi Kushner to read biblical Hebrew. I was delighted to find the Hebrew punchy, colloquial, and magnificent—the transcription of the oral traditions of a voluble people.

The King James Bible is the touchstone of all subsequent English. Its cadences are found in the speeches of Churchill, of Lincoln, of Mark Twain, and, unfortunately, in the pompous utterances of the current politician.

It is plagal, measured, rhythmic, and very much informed by Western musical tradition.

The rhythm of its language is the accepted form of the utterance of authority. But the original Hebrew, the document which has formed the consciousness of the Jews, is neither plagal nor portentous. It is the language of legend—the language of the storyteller, of the campsite: "she saw him and she fell off her camel," "he was comforted, after the death of his mother," "And then there was a new King, and he didn't know this Joseph," "And Esau sobbed to his father, 'Bless me, Me, too. . . .' "

Everything in the world belongs to God, except the Torah. The Torah belongs to us.

It is authority, but it does not speak with the voice of authority; it speaks with the beautiful voice of tradition and allows us the authority to accept and understand—like a good teacher.

וַיִּגְדְּלוּ הַנְּעָרִים וַיְהִי עֵשָׂו אִישׁ יֹדֵעַ צַיִד אִישׁ שָׂדֶה
וְיַעֲקֹב אִישׁ תָּם יֹשֵׁב אֹהָלִים: וַיֶּאֱהַב יִצְחָק אֶת־עֵשָׂו
כִּי־צַיִד בְּפִיו וְרִבְקָה אֹהֶבֶת אֶת־יַעֲקֹב: וַיָּזֶד יַעֲקֹב נָזִיד
וַיָּבֹא עֵשָׂו מִן־הַשָּׂדֶה וְהוּא עָיֵף: וַיֹּאמֶר עֵשָׂו
אֶל־יַעֲקֹב הַלְעִיטֵנִי נָא מִן־הָאָדֹם הָאָדֹם הַזֶּה כִּי עָיֵף
אָנֹכִי עַל־כֵּן קָרָא־שְׁמוֹ אֱדוֹם: וַיֹּאמֶר יַעֲקֹב מִכְרָה
כַיּוֹם אֶת־בְּכֹרָתְךָ לִי:

nd so the boys grew up. Red [that is, Esau] became a hunter, a man of the outdoors, but Sly [that is, Jacob] was a pure soul who liked to stay at home. Isaac loved Red because he had a taste for game, but Rebecca loved Sly. Once, when Sly was cooking up some porridge, Red came in from the field famished. Red said to Sly, "Please let me have a little of this red, red stuff because I am famished"—that's why his name is Red. But Sly said, "Only if you sell me your right as a firstborn son."

Deprived of being able to own farmland, Jews became urban. Required to loan money on interest, they became bankers. Forbidden to own guns, they became pacifists. And outnumbered, they learned not to pick fights. On virtually every front, for two millennia, Jews renounced all things physical, from combat to prowess, taking their refuge instead in the power of mind, or what Heschel called the universe of time. We would survive with the cunning of intellect. Then, when the Holocaust demonstrated the folly of powerlessness, the people of Israel built the state of Israel and turned everything upside down. And the myth—it was always only a few biblical lines refracted through rabbinic tradition—of Sly and Red, Jacob and Esau, Jew and gentile, Jerusalem and Rome, was finally broken. A new generation of Israel now identifies with Esau's power as much as Jacob's intellect. But, to paraphrase the great Israeli novelist A. B. Yehoshua, having to do two thousand years of cramming in just fifty years, we Israelis are still a little new and awkward at it. As a culture and a religious tradition, Jews have yet to balance the archetypes of mind and body, morality and power. We would do well to remember that the brothers began as twins in the same womb.

In *Bereshit*, we see the waters beneath separated from the waters above by the *rakia*, or firmament. Here is an intuition, or immanent knowledge, of the division of the first cell. The progress of life, the cooling of the earth, the retreat of the waters, the fish becoming the landborne mammals, which evolve into humankind—these are the birth memories of the human race.

Adam and Eve dwell in *Gan Eden* in a state of blissful infancy; they live instinctually, free of worry, and so (symbolically, at least) free from want.

The attainment of self-consciousness banishes them from the infant world, and begets the various trials which we find reported and predicted in the *Humash*, and which continue to inform our daily lives.

The struggle between Esau and Jacob denotes the break between the nomad and the agrarian. Esau is a man of the hunt, while Jacob liked to linger at home.

Esau is happy until he encounters duplicity and betrayal—he lives in nature, and, depicted as the "hairy man," is in fact as connected to the beasts as to humanity.

His tragic betrayal, his incomprehension, and his pathetic entreaties—first to his brother, and then to their father—"Bless me, too"—depict, as does the story of *Gan Eden*, a memory of infancy. Jacob's betrayal of his brother recapitulates Eve's disobedience—it is a dramatic and *irrevocable* rift. One is barred from return to the Garden; Jacob and Esau cannot be reconciled. Our human evolution will continue, in the Torah and in the rest of our life, according to a divine and unknowable plan.

What can we do but weep with the Hebrew Bible. "Bless me, too."

וַיִּיקַץ יַעֲקֹב מִשְּׁנָתוֹ וַיֹּאמֶר אָכֵן יֵשׁ יְהוָֹה בַּמָּקוֹם הַזֶּה
וְאָנֹכִי לֹא יָדָעְתִּי: וַיִּירָא וַיֹּאמַר מַה־נּוֹרָא הַמָּקוֹם הַזֶּה
אֵין זֶה כִּי אִם־בֵּית אֱלֹקִים וְזֶה שַׁעַר הַשָּׁמָיִם: וַיַּשְׁכֵּם
יַעֲקֹב בַּבֹּקֶר וַיִּקַּח אֶת־הָאֶבֶן אֲשֶׁר־שָׂם מְרַאֲשֹׁתָיו
וַיָּשֶׂם אֹתָהּ מַצֵּבָה וַיִּצֹק שֶׁמֶן עַל־רֹאשָׁהּ: וַיִּקְרָא
אֶת־שֵׁם־הַמָּקוֹם הַהוּא בֵּית־אֵל וְאוּלָם לוּז שֵׁם־הָעִיר
לָרִאשֹׁנָה:

And Jacob awoke from his sleep and he said, "Surely God was in this place and me; I didn't even know it!" And he was overcome with reverence and said, "How awesome is this place; this is the very house of God and this is the gateway to heaven!" And Jacob awoke in the morning and took the stone that had been under his head and set it up as a marker and anointed it with oil. And he called the name of that place, that used to be called Luz, "Beit Ael, the House of God."

I n Song of Songs 5:2, we read, "I was asleep but my heart was awake." What is it about ordinary, waking consciousness that seems to filter out experiences of the sacred? We intuit that something more must be out there, but in order to see it, we have to close our eyes. Our nights, on the other hand, are often cluttered with holy encounters—inspiring *and* terrifying. But they always seem to remain just beyond reach, inaccessible, their content either ephemeral or opaque.

Jacob's dream is probably the most powerful and transformative personal encounter with the divine in the entire Torah. Equally noteworthy is that the event must be anchored in *waking* reality. Jacob does this by setting up a pile of rocks to mark the spot. And, because even the memory of such an experience is so slippery, the one who received it must establish the place, mark the coordinates in ordinary space. And so Jacob sets up a memorial to something that happened *in the night* and names it the *dwelling place of God*.

T he child must be spared adult interpretation. The morality play, the cautionary tale, and the "educational" children's book exist, and the child understands them to exist, for the purpose of buttressing authority. The gentle indirections of art, of education, of religion, whose first purpose is an avowal of love, and whose secondary purpose is the transmission of information—these, on the other hand, are a precious base upon which the individual might begin to construct his or her own education.

What could be more pointed or more moving than the *Kol Nidre* declaration: ". . . as per the court on high, and as per the court below, it is decreed that tonight it is permitted to pray with sinners."

Similarly, we consign the final grains of *hametz* to the fire, before *Pesah*, and most gratefully recite the absolving prayer, "This represents all the *hametz* under my control—known or unknown."

These traditions, whether we understand them to be divine writ, divine inspiration, or of human construction, remind us that little is in our control, that we are fallible, that we are prone to sin, and *will* sin, even in the service of the divine, and that it has been foreseen and understood.

Jacob, even in the heat of divine revelation, could only be human—and he anointed a stone.

וַיִּוָּתֵר יַעֲקֹב לְבַדּוֹ וַיֵּאָבֵק אִישׁ עִמּוֹ עַד עֲלוֹת הַשָּׁחַר: וַיַּרְא כִּי לֹא יָכֹל לוֹ וַיִּגַּע בְּכַף־יְרֵכוֹ וַתֵּקַע כַּף־יֶרֶךְ יַעֲקֹב בְּהֵאָבְקוֹ עִמּוֹ: וַיֹּאמֶר שַׁלְּחֵנִי כִּי עָלָה הַשָּׁחַר וַיֹּאמֶר לֹא אֲשַׁלֵּחֲךָ כִּי אִם־בֵּרַכְתָּנִי: וַיֹּאמֶר אֵלָיו מַה־שְּׁמֶךָ וַיֹּאמֶר יַעֲקֹב: וַיֹּאמֶר לֹא יַעֲקֹב יֵאָמֵר עוֹד שִׁמְךָ כִּי אִם־יִשְׂרָאֵל כִּי־שָׂרִיתָ עִם־אֱלֹקִים וְעִם־אֲנָשִׁים וַתּוּכָל:

And Jacob was left alone, and someone wrestled with him until the break of dawn. And he saw that he was not up to it. And he hit Jacob in the groin, and the hollow of Jacob's thigh was strained as he wrestled with him. And he said, "Let me go, dawn is breaking." And he said, "I won't let you go until you bless me." And he said to him, "What's your name?" And he said, "Jacob." And he said, "Jacob will no longer be your name, but Israel, because you have struggled with God and with human beings and have survived."

I t's a struggle between Jacob, intent on transcending the ignominy of his past and the *sitra akhra* (the other side), intent on wounding him with it. Apparently, Jacob's nameless adversary has power only in the darkness of night. But this dark side of creation's psyche can also bestow new names, victorious and healing ones. Light and darkness; good and evil; life and death. Perhaps it's no accident that the Jewish Book of the Dead is called *Ma'avar Yabok* (The Ford at the Jabok). That's where the struggle happens, at a place where the river is shallow; if you're careful, you can make it back and forth.

Commentators have long disagreed over the identity of the unnamed wrestler and over just whose agent he was. Did he serve God—after all, he does confer the blessing of a new name—or does he work for Esau, the enemy, the dark side? The correct answer may be "Yes, both of the above." The dark side has always been in the employ of the Holy One just as the reality of God necessarily includes darkness and other horrors. And just this is Jacob's resolution, his transformation into Israel: that God is not just one *or* the other. God is both.

And the man wrestled with him until the break of dawn," or "What shall we give the Sun God?"

Anxiety is a fact of life. Pagans, Druids, Christians, and Jews grow anxious at the disappearance of the Sun in December. The Pagans indulged in ritual sacrifice, an act of appeasement to the angry, and departing, Power. Christians celebrate Christmas; Jews, our own Festival of Light. Modern "scientific" man calls December anxiety "depression" and attributes it to the lack of photostimulus.

The phenomenon—a feeling of unease-anxiety-depression-sadness—can be described by different names, on different levels of abstraction, and addressed through differing mechanisms.

Late-winter "blahs" may be alleviated by the chocolate of Valentine's Day, the alcohol of Purim, or the sun of a trip to the Tropics.

Nonspecific anxiety—free-floating anxiety—in addition to being the purview of (to name a few) the spiritualist, the confidence artist, the psychoanalytic establishment, the self-help movement, is also addressed by religion.

The Doctrine of Original Sin puts a name on (and so ameliorates) anomie; a similar result is achieved through racial hatred. ("Aha. I now see that my unease was caused by the Jews, the Blacks, etc.")

Sacrifice—of a human being, of self-esteem, of oxen and sheep, of anything of worth—is a traditional, effective (if temporary) specific for anomie.

But the relationship of Jews to God is defined by the *Akedah*—by the *renunciation of sacrifice*. With the fall of the Temple, animal sacrifice (human sacrifice *manqué*) disappeared.

We Jews were left with the *question of how to serve God.* Anxiety, now, could be stilled only through prayer, *mitzvot,* study.

The relationship of Jews to God is defined also through Jacob's struggle with the angel. Many Jews since have been "up all night struggling." It is not that we struggle *more* than other groups—anxiety is a part of the human condition, and distributed equally to all—but that, absent, and having, in fact, *renounced* sacrifice, we are, perhaps, left *more aware of the struggle.*

The term "Jewish guilt" is a racial derogation. It is not that Jews are "guilty" (what have we to be guilty of?), but that the *Akedah* (like the Tree of Knowledge of Good and Evil) blesses us with the task of seeking self-knowledge, which task necessarily entails upon the seeker anxiety and doubt.

To reconfigure this legitimate if unsettling worldview into *guilt* is, in effect, a return to barred practices of sacrifice—in this case the sacrifice is not of a life, but of self-respect.

וַיִּמְצָאֵהוּ אִישׁ וְהִנֵּה תֹעֶה בַּשָּׂדֶה וַיִּשְׁאָלֵהוּ הָאִישׁ
לֵאמֹר מַה־תְּבַקֵּשׁ: וַיֹּאמֶר אֶת־אַחַי אָנֹכִי מְבַקֵּשׁ
הַגִּידָה־נָּא לִי אֵיפֹה הֵם רֹעִים: וַיֹּאמֶר הָאִישׁ נָסְעוּ
מִזֶּה כִּי שָׁמַעְתִּי אֹמְרִים נֵלְכָה דֹּתָיְנָה וַיֵּלֶךְ יוֹסֵף אַחַר
אֶחָיו וַיִּמְצָאֵם בְּדֹתָן: וַיִּרְאוּ אֹתוֹ מֵרָחֹק וּבְטֶרֶם יִקְרַב
אֲלֵיהֶם וַיִּתְנַכְּלוּ אֹתוֹ לַהֲמִיתוֹ: וַיֹּאמְרוּ אִישׁ אֶל־אָחִיו
הִנֵּה בַּעַל הַחֲלֹמוֹת הַלָּזֶה בָּא:

A man found him wandering in the field and the man asked him, "What are you looking for?" And he said, "I'm trying to find my brothers. Could you tell me where they're pasturing?" And the man said, "They've left here, for I overheard them say: 'Let's go to Dothan.'" So Joseph set out after his brothers and found them in Dothan. They saw him from a distance and, before he got close to them, they conspired to kill him. They said to one another, "Behold, here comes that dreamer!"

The Joseph novella, the last thirteen chapters of the book of Genesis, may be the first modern piece of literature. Nowhere in it does God say or do anything. Through Joseph's awful descent into Egyptian slavery and his equally dizzying ascent to the Egyptian throne, God apparently does nothing. Br'er Rabbit, he lay low. All the characters in the saga remain convinced that they are controlling their own destinies, busily going about their own business, completing what they believe are their own agendas. But we who have read the story countless times know better. We understand that the whole thing is just one big setup to get the Jewish people living (what they think will be) happily every after in Egypt at the end of Genesis and (blissfully) unaware of the advent of some evil pharaoh who won't remember Joseph and his brothers. But evidence of divine (albeit anonymous) manipulation abounds. Perhaps one of the most compelling examples is the unnamed stranger who meets Joseph and tells him where his brothers (and destiny) await. "I just coincidentally overheard them say they were headed toward Dothan," he says. Now if we were to be given such a line in modern literature, we would balk at the whole thing. "Artificial, clumsy, plot contrivance," we'd complain. Surely the author can come up with a better way to get Joseph to his conniving brothers without resorting to some anonymous tip. Why not just send him to Dothan in the first place? What possible literary value could there be in this irrelevant side trip to the field of Shechem? Nothing at all except, perhaps, getting the reader to wonder about why there are seemingly irrelevant side trips occasionally populated by unnamed strangers whose words change everything.

DM

How does the man know Joseph's identity? How in the world does he know who Joseph's brothers might be? Joseph does not name himself, nor does he describe his brothers. Neither does he ask, "Do you know where they might be?" He says, "Have the goodness to tell me where they are."

To whom is he speaking?

Traditional interpretation would say an angel or messenger; psychoanalytic thought might say "an aspect of himself" (i.e., he *externalizes* the ability to recognize the difficult: that his brothers are gone from him). In each case, whether through the "messenger," (an extension of God to the self) or through the unconscious, as an extension of the self toward "wholeness" (i.e., God), a bridge is being made—a bridge to the *spiritual*. Joseph's problems were beyond his understanding (how to be at peace with his brothers), and were not cured nor addressed by, his understanding. They were solved by religion.

וַיִּשְׁלַח פַּרְעֹה וַיִּקְרָא אֶת־יוֹסֵף וַיְרִיצֻהוּ מִן־הַבּוֹר וַיְגַלַּח
וַיְחַלֵּף שִׂמְלֹתָיו וַיָּבֹא אֶל־פַּרְעֹה: וַיֹּאמֶר פַּרְעֹה
אֶל־יוֹסֵף חֲלוֹם חָלַמְתִּי וּפֹתֵר אֵין אֹתוֹ וַאֲנִי שָׁמַעְתִּי
עָלֶיךָ לֵאמֹר תִּשְׁמַע חֲלוֹם לִפְתֹּר אֹתוֹ: וַיַּעַן יוֹסֵף
אֶת־פַּרְעֹה לֵאמֹר בִּלְעָדָי אֱלֹקִים יַעֲנֶה אֶת־שְׁלוֹם
פַּרְעֹה: וַיְדַבֵּר פַּרְעֹה אֶל־יוֹסֵף בַּחֲלֹמִי הִנְנִי עֹמֵד
עַל־שְׂפַת הַיְאֹר:

And Pharaoh sent and summoned Joseph. They hurried him up from the dungeon, gave him a shave, changed his clothes, and brought him to Pharaoh. Pharaoh said to Joseph, "I have dreamed a dream but I don't know what it means. Now I have heard it said about you that for you to hear a dream is to interpret it." And Joseph answered Pharaoh, saying, "Not I, but God will respond to Pharaoh's peace of mind." And Pharaoh said to Joseph, "In my dream, behold I was standing on the bank of the Nile."

By interpreting all three sets of double dreams, Joseph is able to accurately foretell the future. But the only good it does him is to seal his destiny. The first time, his dreams get him sold into slavery. The second, his interpretations establish his reputation. And the third, he's made king of Egypt. The act of dreaming (or interpreting) the future only seals it!

The Hebrew word for "dungeon" here is *bor,* or pit, the same word used to describe the cistern into which Joseph was thrown by his brothers (back in Genesis 37:24). There the obvious meaning of his own two dreams (sheaves, then planets bow down to him) gets him thrown into a *bor.* Now his astonishingly accurate interpretation of the baker's and the butler's dreams gets Pharaoh to raise him *up* from the *bor,* the dungeon.

The first pit shows up again in *Midrash Tanhuma.* The whole family has settled in Goshen and Jacob has died. In accordance with their father's wish, the brothers bury him in Canaan. As they are returning to Egypt, Joseph leaves the caravan for a short time but unaware he is under the secret surveillance of Simeon and Levi. When they follow him to the same pit they once intended to be his grave, they are horrified and certain that, now that their father is dead, Joseph will finally take his vengeance on them. If they had been within earshot, however, the *midrash* explains, they would only have overheard him recite a simple blessing: "Praised are You, O God, who has done a miracle for me in this place!"

DM

Pharaoh asks Joseph as Joseph asks the man in *Vayashev*. Both, in extremity, reach out to the lowly. The terminal patient seeks out the medicine man, the distraught traveler pours out his heart to the stranger.

The operative mechanism is that of the rabbinic injunction: that the distressed can apply to any rabbi for direction, but that, having chosen, he must abide by the rabbi's words.

This mechanism functions, also, in the traditional choice of the Jew as the advisor to the throne (cf. Joseph, Henry Kissinger, Benjamin Disraeli, Madeleine Albright, Barry Goldwater, etc.), in which the body politic unconsciously selects a person historically deemed to be disinterested (i.e., not of the tribe).

וְעַתָּה יֵשֶׁב־נָא עַבְדְּךָ תַּחַת הַנַּעַר עֶבֶד לַאדֹנִי וְהַנַּעַר
יַעַל עִם־אֶחָיו: כִּי־אֵיךְ אֶעֱלֶה אֶל־אָבִי וְהַנַּעַר אֵינֶנּוּ
אִתִּי פֶּן אֶרְאֶה בָרָע אֲשֶׁר יִמְצָא אֶת־אָבִי: וְלֹא־יָכֹל
יוֹסֵף לְהִתְאַפֵּק לְכֹל הַנִּצָּבִים עָלָיו וַיִּקְרָא הוֹצִיאוּ
כָל־אִישׁ מֵעָלָי וְלֹא־עָמַד אִישׁ אִתּוֹ בְּהִתְוַדַּע יוֹסֵף
אֶל־אֶחָיו:

S o now please let your servant remain as my lord's
slave instead of the boy; let the boy go back up with
his brothers. For how can I go back up to my father
if the boy isn't with me? I cannot bear to look upon the
agony that would overcome my father. Joseph could no
longer control himself before all his attendants, and he
cried out: "Get everyone away from me!" Now there was
no one else with him when Joseph made himself known to
his brothers.

LK

Joseph has set this whole scene up. He has framed his only full brother, Benjamin. He has meticulously arranged things so that now all his brothers need to do is report the truth to their father: The kid was literally caught with the goods on him. It's an opportunity for an exact replay of when they threw Joseph in the pit and lied to their father that he had been devoured by a wild beast. This time the man (Joseph) will throw Benjamin into an Egyptian dungeon.

Rabbinic tradition counsels that we don't know if someone has genuinely made atonement for a sin until he or she has an opportunity to commit the same sin again and does not. So now, unbeknownst to them, Joseph has put his brothers to the test. He has even greased the skids this time for them to choose self-interest over sibling. (Or perhaps Joseph is giving his brothers a second chance. How many people would do that for their siblings?) But this time Judah walks right into the jaws of what he must believe is his own slavery. "Take me instead of the boy," he says. And that melts Joseph's heart. Now Joseph could "make himself known" to his brothers.

f you would forgive your enemy, first injure him." Joseph attempts to master his desire for revenge through repetition. He teases and confuses his brothers—he bids them come and go, tests them, accuses them falsely, and puts them in mortal fear.

Throughout their visits, the impulse toward cruel revenge is weakened, allowing his sorrow to emerge.

Contrast a tradition which counsels to "turn the other cheek."

The Torah acknowledges that unpleasant and destructive feelings cannot be wished away, they must be examined and dealt with.

Joseph takes revenge symbolically, but it is restorative nonetheless. It allows him to weep and he is cleansed.

We find the same mechanism in the surprise party, in the old Boxing Day custom of having the servants and masters exchange clothes, in the office party, where the inferior employees, licensed by alcohol, can "tell the boss the Truth."

The "other men," whom Joseph sends out of the room, may be seen to be conflicting impulses (what else are advisors?). They are banished, allowing Joseph to acknowledge that (for the moment) he is moved to wholeness, that he can put aside both revenge and reason, and be reduced to distraction and sorrow and love.

12. GENESIS 50:18–20 / VAYEHI

וַיֵּלְכוּ גַּם־אֶחָיו וַיִּפְּלוּ לְפָנָיו וַיֹּאמְרוּ הִנֶּנּוּ לְךָ לַעֲבָדִים:
וַיֹּאמֶר אֲלֵהֶם יוֹסֵף אַל־תִּירָאוּ כִּי הֲתַחַת אֱלֹקִים אָנִי:
וְאַתֶּם חֲשַׁבְתֶּם עָלַי רָעָה אֱלֹקִים חֲשָׁבָהּ לְטֹבָה לְמַעַן
עֲשֹׂה כַּיּוֹם הַזֶּה לְהַחֲיֹת עַם־רָב:

And also his brothers came, and they fell on their faces before him and they said, "Behold, we are your servants." But Joseph said: "Don't be afraid. Am I God? You planned evil against me but God planned good in order to bring about what has happened today, the saving of many people."

Even at the end of the novella, Joseph's brothers are still in the dark. They remain convinced they can manipulate the outcome of the plot and their own destinies. Thirteen chapters of Genesis earlier (chapter 37) (and over two decades, by the story's counting), they figured they could be rid of Joseph by throwing him into a pit. Now that Joseph is on the throne, they figure they can ensure their own safety by claiming they're ready to be his servants. They still don't understand that the whole thing— from Joseph's coat of many colors to his royal robes— has all been part of some larger plan that God has for the Jewish people. Joseph alone seems to understand: Everything has conspired to bring them into Egypt.

We, who have rehearsed the story countless times since childhood, know even more. By next week's *parasha*, a new king will arise over Egypt who will not remember Joseph and his brothers. He will set task masters over Israel. And the Jewish people will be enslaved for four hundred years. Only then will God do business with us. The slavery, we realize, is apparently a didactic precondition of our mission. And, while Joseph certainly does not foresee that, even now he does comprehend how human plans evaporate in the presence of God's plan. Joseph sits up there on that throne remembering his dreams and the pit, Ms. Potiphar and the dungeon, Pharaoh's dreams and the famine, and he understands. Something else is going on and coming down. It is much bigger than isolated human agendas and connivings. As the old Yiddish proverb has it, man plans, God laughs. What a fitting conclusion to Genesis and bridge to the book of Exodus.

DM

To question the existence of the Shoah is a heinous, anti-Semitic act. In some countries it is, indeed, a crime.

But someday the existence of the Shoah will be debated—even by Jews—just as, today, some debate the historical reality of the Egyptian bondage. At that future date, perhaps thousands of years hence, we Jews ourselves may say, "It is, of course, not possible that our people could undergo such savagery—the entire world turned against us, in arms or apathy—and survive. Surely this is but a hyperbolic and chilling metaphor."

In that far-off debate, other voices will defend the historical reality of this tragedy, and, in so doing, the power of God, and the power of the Jewish people, will endure and wise heads will say that in the storm of the Shoah we see Man intended one thing, but unquestionably God intended something else.

These wise Jews will try to find—*in the debate itself*—beginning of new wisdom.

Such debates and speculation link us both historically—to Jews studying this *parasha* this week—and
vertically, or perhaps circularly, both to notional
Jews of time to come, and to our biblical ancestors.

The ineradicable persistence of the mechanism of
debate both ensures and, one might say, defines our
existence—as if, as is arguably the case, our people
were not the prime movers, but the intended and essential *adjunct* of some celestial debate.

We analyze a dream, and if we are persistent, new
unforseeable elements arise. They are rejected, they
reappear, then recast our entire understanding. Perhaps we are indeed thoughts in the mind of God. We
struggle with each other and ourselves in an attempt
to recast the judgment.

EXODUS / *SHEMOT*

וּמֹשֶׁה הָיָה רֹעֶה אֶת־צֹאן יִתְרוֹ חֹתְנוֹ כֹּהֵן מִדְיָן וַיִּנְהַג
אֶת־הַצֹּאן אַחַר הַמִּדְבָּר וַיָּבֹא אֶל־הַר הָאֱלֹקִים
חֹרֵבָה: וַיֵּרָא מַלְאַךְ יְדֹוָד אֵלָיו בְּלַבַּת־אֵשׁ מִתּוֹךְ
הַסְּנֶה וַיַּרְא וְהִנֵּה הַסְּנֶה בֹּעֵר בָּאֵשׁ וְהַסְּנֶה אֵינֶנּוּ
אֻכָּל: וַיֹּאמֶר מֹשֶׁה אָסֻרָה־נָּא וְאֶרְאֶה אֶת־הַמַּרְאֶה
הַגָּדֹל הַזֶּה מַדּוּעַ לֹא־יִבְעַר הַסְּנֶה: וַיַּרְא יְדֹוָד כִּי סָר
לִרְאוֹת וַיִּקְרָא אֵלָיו אֱלֹקִים מִתּוֹךְ הַסְּנֶה וַיֹּאמֶר מֹשֶׁה
מֹשֶׁה וַיֹּאמֶר הִנֵּנִי: וַיֹּאמֶר אַל־תִּקְרַב הֲלֹם שַׁל־נְעָלֶיךָ
מֵעַל רַגְלֶיךָ כִּי הַמָּקוֹם אֲשֶׁר אַתָּה עוֹמֵד עָלָיו
אַדְמַת־קֹדֶשׁ הוּא:

Now Moses was tending the flock of Jethro, his father-in-law, the priest of Midian, and he led the flock to the far edge of the wilderness and he came to the mountain of God, to Horeb. And a messenger of God appeared to him in a blazing fire from out of a bush. And he looked and, behold: A bush was burning but the bush was not consumed. Moses said, "I must turn aside to look at this incredible sight: Why doesn't the bush burn up?" And when God saw that he had turned aside to look, God called to him from out of the bush: "Moses! Moses!" And he answered, "Here am I." And He said, "Do not come closer. Remove your sandals from your feet, for the place on which you are standing is holy ground."

D espite the grazing flock, this is hardly a pastoral scene. Something is strangely on fire. "And Moses hid his face for he was afraid to look at God" (Exodus 3:6). Even the name of the mountain is Horeb, from the Hebrew, meaning "to be destroyed or ravaged."

The whole scene is itself a prototype of what will come when Moses brings the Jewish people back here. There will be fire too, but then it will engulf the whole mountain: "Now Mount Sinai was all in smoke, for the Lord had come down upon it in fire. . . . Warn the people not to break through to the Lord to gaze, lest many of them perish" (Exodus 19:18, 21). Dangerous business here. You get too close, you see too much, you could get fried.

But that only makes us want to know: if something is being shown to Moses, can he—or anyone—look without being destroyed? (How strangely fitting that the final verses of Deuteronomy describe Moses as the only person who ever saw God face-to-face! [Deuteronomy 34:10])

Perhaps it was never meant to be an attention-grabbing miracle. Maybe the bush is a metaphor for the self, aflame with the presence of God that miraculously is not consumed. Everything we know tells us that such moments of rapture should destroy us. The mystery of the bush that burns but is not consumed comes to teach us otherwise. Indeed, it happens all the time. Professor Alexander Altmann once observed, "Finding God and worshipping [God] is but another way of saying that we have found our Self . . . [We are] spiritually reborn in God, and God is, as it were, reborn in [us]."

Now we understand God's instruction. "Remove your sandals from your feet, for the place on which you stand is holy ground" (Exodus 3:5). It's everywhere.

DM

The Scots, in times of difficulty, "took to the heather." The French resistants, the maquisards, were named for the maquis, or heather, which hid them.

The s'neh or "shrub" of the burning bush (the presumed root of Sinai) was and continues to be the refuge of another minority group.

וַיְדַבֵּר אֱלֹקִים אֶל־מֹשֶׁה וַיֹּאמֶר אֵלָיו אֲנִי יְדֹוָד: וָאֵרָא
אֶל־אַבְרָהָם אֶל־יִצְחָק וְאֶל־יַעֲקֹב בְּאֵל שַׁדָּי וּשְׁמִי
יְדֹוָד   לֹא נוֹדַעְתִּי לָהֶם: וְגַם הֲקִמֹתִי אֶת־בְּרִיתִי אִתָּם
לָתֵת לָהֶם אֶת־אֶרֶץ כְּנַעַן אֵת אֶרֶץ מְגֻרֵיהֶם
אֲשֶׁר־גָּרוּ בָהּ: וְגַם אֲנִי שָׁמַעְתִּי אֶת־נַאֲקַת בְּנֵי יִשְׂרָאֵל
אֲשֶׁר מִצְרַיִם מַעֲבִדִים אֹתָם וָאֶזְכֹּר אֶת־בְּרִיתִי:

And God spoke to Moses and said to him,
"I am Adonai. I appeared to Abraham, Isaac,
and Jacob as El Shaddai, but, by My name
Adonai, I did not make Myself known to them. I also established My covenant with them, to give them the land of
Canaan, the land in which they dwelt as sojourners. And
now I have heard the crying of the Israelites because the
Egyptians are holding them in bondage. And I have remembered My covenant."

Only a few chapters ago, God finally revealed God's Name to Moses. In what must surely be one of the slipperiest answers of all time, God says: "You want to know my Name? Okay, My Name is 'I'll be whoever I'll be' " (Exodus 3:14).

That's not a name, it's a handful of smoke and mirrors! ("Pay no attention to that man behind the screen!" insists the Wizard of Oz.)

My own parents each had different names for God. My mother's was constant, unchanging, sure. God may have been whoever God wanted to be, but God somehow always wanted to remain the same. The God her father received from his parents was the same one she gave to me. My father's God was a different story. The youngest of eight, he never even knew much about his own parents, let alone their God. Sometimes God was a player in his life, but just as often the two of them were strangers to one another. His God was intermittent, sporadic, mute.

So now, in our verse, God comes along and announces (after four hundred years without so much as a postcard!) that even though your parents knew me by a different name(s), I've been the same God all along. And furthermore, I'm letting you in on my own name for Myself, a Name made from only vowels, a name made from the root letters of the Hebrew

verb "to be," a Name scholars think must have once
meant "the One who brings into being all that is," a
Name whose pronunciation sounds like breathing.
And, here's the main thing, this name—even though
your parents never knew it—has been my Name all
along. (I'll bet that's what you told them too!) The
goal here seems to be the continuity of God's identity. The Kabbalists say that when the Messiah comes
he or she will teach us how to pronounce the entire
Torah as one long, uninterruptible Name of God.

DM

And God said he had been known as *El Shaddai*,
But henceforward would be called *Yod Hey Vav Hey*—
Why did God change His Name?
"Too Jewish."

15. EXODUS 13:14–16 / BO

וְהָיָה כִּי־יִשְׁאָלְךָ בִנְךָ מָחָר לֵאמֹר מַה־זֹּאת וְאָמַרְתָּ
אֵלָיו בְּחֹזֶק יָד הוֹצִיאָנוּ יְדֹוָד   מִמִּצְרַיִם מִבֵּית עֲבָדִים:
וַיְהִי כִּי־הִקְשָׁה פַרְעֹה לְשַׁלְּחֵנוּ וַיַּהֲרֹג יְדֹוָד   כָּל־בְּכוֹר
בְּאֶרֶץ מִצְרַיִם מִבְּכֹר אָדָם וְעַד־בְּכוֹר בְּהֵמָה עַל־כֵּן
אֲנִי זֹבֵחַ לַיהֹוָד   כָּל־פֶּטֶר רֶחֶם הַזְּכָרִים וְכָל־בְּכוֹר בָּנַי
אֶפְדֶּה: וְהָיָה לְאוֹת עַל־יָדְכָה וּלְטוֹטָפֹת בֵּין עֵינֶיךָ כִּי
בְּחֹזֶק יָד הוֹצִיאָנוּ יְדֹוָד   מִמִּצְרָיִם:

A nd when, in the future, your child asks you
and says, "What's going on?" you shall say
to your child, "With a strong hand God
brought us out of Egypt, from the house of bondage. When
Pharaoh's heart was hardened against letting us leave,
God killed every first-born in the land of Egypt, from the
first-born of human to the first born of beast. Therefore I
now sacrifice to God every first male issue of the womb, but
redeem every first-born among my sons." And so it shall be
for a sign upon your hand and for frontlets between your
eyes that with a strong hand God brought us out from
Egypt.

It's a showdown between God and Pharaoh, a test of fatherhood, a contest between a loving father—who again and again refuses the death of the son in favor of his redemption—and a sclerotic Egyptian despot who thinks he's God. (Remember Yul Brynner in *The Ten Commandments* asking in indignation, "Who is this god?")

Redemption is used in several ways. The slave people are redeemed from bondage in Egypt. On the simplest level, they are cashed in for free men and women. The people are also God's firstborn. They belong to God. (Later, at Sinai, God will produce the pawn ticket: "I bought you, I own you, you owe Me.") Pharaoh kills all the (firstborn) man-children—throws them into the river, feeds them to the crocodiles. But God redeems them just as earthly fathers are bidden to redeem their own sons. Redemption of the Firstborn, *Pidyon haBen.*

But there is still another redemption here. The child asks, "What's going on, Dad?" The father answers, "It was with a mighty hand that the Lord brought us out from Egypt, the house of bondage." And here too, yes, the child is redeemed. A father may, you see, also redeem his son through just recounting the story of how God redeemed him. A parent redeems a child through helping him to remember. Over the entrance to Yad vaShem, Israel's memorial to those who perished in the Holocaust, are the words attributed to the Ba'al Shem Tov: "Memory is the source of redemption."

DM

The Hebrew text states *not* that Pharaoh hardened himself to again deny the Jews, but that he *hardened himself to let us go,* and that HaShem, in response, slew all his firstborn.

At the risk of a homiletic, perhaps Pharaoh's action was that of the self-congratulatory philanthropist, well-wisher, liberal, bleeding heart, pick-your-own-epithet, who, having made a difficult, costly choice, pats himself on the back, regroups and recruits himself for a (generally lengthy, and frequently infinite) period before its implementation.

So: Pharaoh hardened himself to let the Jewish people go, and HaShem slew the firstborn. For the decision itself was nothing laudable—Pharaoh had so decided before—and resolution itself is nothing. Without action, it is self-worshipping fantasy.

וַיֹּאמֶר מֹשֶׁה אֶל־הָעָם אַל־תִּירָאוּ הִתְיַצְּבוּ וּרְאוּ
אֶת־יְשׁוּעַת יְדֹוָד אֲשֶׁר־יַעֲשֶׂה לָכֶם הַיּוֹם כִּי אֲשֶׁר
רְאִיתֶם אֶת־מִצְרַיִם הַיּוֹם לֹא תֹסִפוּ לִרְאֹתָם עוֹד
עַד־עוֹלָם: יְדֹוָד יִלָּחֵם לָכֶם וְאַתֶּם תַּחֲרִשׁוּן: וַיֹּאמֶר
יְדֹוָד אֶל־מֹשֶׁה מַה־תִּצְעַק אֵלָי דַּבֵּר אֶל־בְּנֵי־יִשְׂרָאֵל
וְיִסָּעוּ: וְאַתָּה הָרֵם אֶת־מַטְּךָ וּנְטֵה אֶת־יָדְךָ עַל־הַיָּם
וּבְקָעֵהוּ וְיָבֹאוּ בְנֵי־יִשְׂרָאֵל בְּתוֹךְ הַיָּם בַּיַּבָּשָׁה:

D o not be afraid! Stand your ground and witness
the salvation which God will do for you today.
For the Egyptians whom you see today you will
never see again. God will do battle for you. Hold your
peace!" Then God said to Moses, "Why are you crying
out to Me? Tell the Israelites to go forward. Lift up your
staff and hold out your arm over the sea and split it, so the
Israelites may march into the midst of the sea on dry
ground."

So Israelites follow Moses and his God only to wind up between the approaching Egyptian chariots and the abyss of the Red Sea. Now there is no turning back, no moving forward.

It is logically impossible; cannot be done. You can either be "in the midst of the sea," or you can be "on dry ground." But you cannot, at the same time, be both. The Hasidic master Dov Baer of Mezritch teaches that there is a place, an order of being, called *Ayin*, Nothingness, through which anyone (or anything) must pass before it can become something new. Just a split second after it is no longer what it was but before it is what it would become. This is a place of great terror. When you enter the Nothingness, there can be no guarantees. All bets are off. You could become anything—or remain nothing, forever. Such a place contains both a thing *and* its opposite: Sea *and* dry ground. Life *and* death. Good *and* evil. Slavery *and* freedom.

You want to know what happened at the sea? I'll tell you. The waters didn't literally split. The people all walked into the sea and drowned. Then they all walked up onto the opposite shore, reborn into free men and women. Into the *Ayin*. . . .

The Egyptians you see today you will never see again"—or, as Freud said: The only way to forget is to remember—you may be beset by other difficulties, but if you address these before you now, you will be free of them. If you repress the necessity, they will accompany you forever.

אָנֹכִי יְדֹוָד אֱלֹהֶיךָ אֲשֶׁר הוֹצֵאתִיךָ מֵאֶרֶץ מִצְרַיִם
מִבֵּית עֲבָדִים: לֹא־יִהְיֶה לְךָ אֱלֹהִים אֲחֵרִים עַל־פָּנָי:
לֹא־תַעֲשֶׂה לְךָ פֶסֶל וְכָל־תְּמוּנָה אֲשֶׁר בַּשָּׁמַיִם מִמַּעַל
וַאֲשֶׁר בָּאָרֶץ מִתָּחַת וַאֲשֶׁר בַּמַּיִם מִתַּחַת לָאָרֶץ:
לֹא־תִשְׁתַּחֲוֶה לָהֶם וְלֹא תָעָבְדֵם כִּי אָנֹכִי יְדֹוָד אֱלֹהֶיךָ
אֵל קַנָּא פֹּקֵד עֲוֹן אָבֹת עַל־בָּנִים עַל־שִׁלֵּשִׁים
וְעַל־רִבֵּעִים לְשֹׂנְאָי: וְעֹשֶׂה חֶסֶד לַאֲלָפִים לְאֹהֲבַי
וּלְשֹׁמְרֵי מִצְוֹתָי:

I the Lord am your God who brought you out of the land
of Egypt, the house of bondage: You shall have no other
gods before Me. You shall not make for yourself a
graven image, or any likeness of what is in the heavens
above, or on the earth below, or in the waters beneath the
earth. You shall not bow down to them or serve them. For I
the Lord your God am a jealous God visiting the guilt of
the parents upon the children, to the third and to the fourth
generations of those who reject Me, but showing kindness
to the thousandth generation of those who love Me and
keep My commandments.

To speak the pronoun "I" is to announce the existence of one's self and thereby claim that all the contradictory, disjointed, cockamamie thoughts, feelings, and actions are all manifestations of one underlying self. "Yes, I know, on the surface, none of it makes sense, but it's all I. It is who I am."

In just this way, the first word God utters to the assembled Israelites at Sinai is therefore that the universe too has a self. All the broken, stupid, hurtful, apparently senseless things that happen in the world are likewise the manifestation of some greater Self. According to some traditions, that "I" contains the seed of all subsequent revelation. That's all God needs to say: "I." The universe has a Self. Indeed, since Hebrew lacks the verb "to be" in the present tense, we could read the first utterance, not as "I am the Lord your God" but " 'I' *is* the Lord your God." In the words of Yehuda Aryeh Lieb of Ger, "Each one of Israel beheld the root of his own soul." We might even say that at that moment each one of them met the Self of the Universe, a Self that tolerates and sustains each individual self.

M any of us grew up hearing, and perhaps ascribing to, the notion of "Jewish guilt."

The notion, for all that it may be self-applied, is racist. It takes a universally distributed human condition—worry, anxiety, stress—and singles out a specific group for its derogatory application.

But perhaps there is another component to the phenomenon. Perhaps Jews, culturally, deal with life's inevitable stresses in a culturally specific and quantifiable way.

If so, I would characterize our attempts as motivated not by guilt, but by a feeling of responsibility.

The first words God speaks to us in *Yitro*—God's most frequent self-introduction—are as that power which brought us forth from Egypt, out of slavery. In return we feel, as well we might, an obligation. Not to discharge this debt might indeed cause one anxiety. To ponder means for its discharge might awaken even in the blameless a sense of concern.

וְגֵר לֹא־תוֹנֶה וְלֹא תִלְחָצֶנּוּ כִּי־גֵרִים הֱיִיתֶם בְּאֶרֶץ
מִצְרָיִם: כָּל־אַלְמָנָה וְיָתוֹם לֹא תְעַנּוּן: אִם־עַנֵּה תְעַנֶּה
אֹתוֹ כִּי אִם־צָעֹק יִצְעַק אֵלַי שָׁמֹעַ אֶשְׁמַע צַעֲקָתוֹ:
וְחָרָה אַפִּי וְהָרַגְתִּי אֶתְכֶם בֶּחָרֶב וְהָיוּ נְשֵׁיכֶם אַלְמָנוֹת
וּבְנֵיכֶם יְתֹמִים: אִם־כֶּסֶף תַּלְוֶה אֶת־עַמִּי אֶת־הֶעָנִי
עִמָּךְ לֹא־תִהְיֶה לוֹ כְּנֹשֶׁה לֹא־תְשִׂימוּן עָלָיו נֶשֶׁךְ:

You shall not wrong a stranger or oppress him,
for you were strangers in the land of Egypt.
You shall not mistreat any widow or orphan.
If you do mistreat them, I will hear their cry when they cry
out to Me, and I will be furious and put you to the sword,
so that your own wives shall become widows and your
own children orphans. If you lend money to My people, to
the poor of your people—do be to him a creditor; exact no
interest from him.

LK

It would be forgivable if we permitted ourselves the solace of dwelling on our victimization as slaves in Egypt. It was horrific; we have every reason to memorialize the terror, bask in the moral luxury of our ancient bondage. But instead, we celebrate it. We transform it, reshape it into the most frequently repeated explanation for any law in the entire Torah— over and over again. Our slavery, instead of embittering us, generates an obligation to identify with anyone who is socially powerless or politically disenfranchised. "You were strangers in the land of Egypt."

DM

So much of the Torah's language is part of our American self-understanding—the widows and orphans of this *parasha* are found in Lincoln's second inaugural address. The fiery swift sword of "The Battle Hymn of the Republic" was originally placed outside the Garden of Eden "and [God] stationed east of the Garden of Eden the cherubim and the fiery, ever-turning sword" (Genesis 3:24). The inscription on the Liberty Bell, "proclaim liberty throughout the land and to all the inhabitants thereof," is found in the Torah as the proclamation of the jubilee year—an announcement of the forgiveness of debt; "God shed His grace on thee," of course, is the unique language of the priestly blessing.

That the songwriters, politicians, and poets may have understood this language—through the King James Bible—as *Christian* is beside the point—we *galut* American Jews, rather than see ourselves as strangers here, can, if so inclined, look to our national love of these "so-American phrases" as the highest—if least conscious—acknowledgment of a debt to the Jews.

וְעָשִׂיתָ שְׁנַיִם כְּרֻבִים זָהָב מִקְשָׁה תַּעֲשֶׂה אֹתָם מִשְּׁנֵי
קְצוֹת הַכַּפֹּרֶת: וַעֲשֵׂה כְּרוּב אֶחָד מִקָּצָה מִזֶּה
וּכְרוּב־אֶחָד מִקָּצָה מִזֶּה מִן־הַכַּפֹּרֶת תַּעֲשׂוּ
אֶת־הַכְּרֻבִים עַל־שְׁנֵי קְצוֹתָיו: וְהָיוּ הַכְּרֻבִים פֹּרְשֵׂי
כְנָפַיִם לְמַעְלָה סֹכְכִים בְּכַנְפֵיהֶם עַל־הַכַּפֹּרֶת וּפְנֵיהֶם
אִישׁ אֶל־אָחִיו אֶל־הַכַּפֹּרֶת יִהְיוּ פְּנֵי הַכְּרֻבִים: וְנָתַתָּ
אֶת־הַכַּפֹּרֶת עַל־הָאָרֹן מִלְמָעְלָה וְאֶל־הָאָרֹן תִּתֵּן
אֶת־הָעֵדֻת אֲשֶׁר אֶתֵּן אֵלֶיךָ: וְנוֹעַדְתִּי לְךָ שָׁם וְדִבַּרְתִּי
אִתְּךָ מֵעַל הַכַּפֹּרֶת מִבֵּין שְׁנֵי הַכְּרֻבִים אֲשֶׁר עַל־אֲרֹן
הָעֵדֻת אֵת כָּל־אֲשֶׁר אֲצַוֶּה אוֹתְךָ אֶל־בְּנֵי יִשְׂרָאֵל:

Make two gold cherubim—make them of hammered work—at both ends of the cover. Make one cherub at one end and another cherub at the other. Make the cherubim at its two ends from the cover. The cherubim shall have their wings spread out above, shielding the cover with their wings. They shall face each other, the faces of the cherubim being turned toward the cover. Set the cover on top of the Ark and inside it place the Pact that I will give you. There I will meet you, and there—from above the cover, between the two cherubim that are on top of the Ark of the Pact—I will speak to you all that I will command you concerning the children of Israel.

For a religious culture obsessed with prohibiting (and obliterating) any graven image, how curious that winged golden statues be set above the Ark. Even more fascinating is the statement that not from inside the Ark nor even from above it, but instead from *between* the statues will God speak. This "in between" the two *cherubim*, two statues, two graven images, is the locus of the voice. As Martin Buber taught us, God is uniquely present in the space in between. And, as the Kabbalists imagined, the *Shekhina*, the feminine, indwelling presence of God, resides between the cherubim.

Neither from one cherub nor the other, but from the space created *between* them—when they confront each other—issues the revelation. Only relationship can initiate life and growth and revelation. And relationship can be created only when one ego realizes that there is another ego of equal importance. It can only be discovered *in the presence of another.* You simply cannot get there alone; there must always be someone else; it takes two to tango.

Perhaps that is why the prohibition against idolatry does not apply here. Truth be told, we are all only lifeless graven images until we face another and, in so doing, bring our selves and the other to life. And from between *that* meeting the divine voice issues.

The Ark of the Covenant and Ezekiel's wheel could both be called fantasy. But the second is a vision, and the first is a divine instruction. To say an instruction is beyond our understanding is not to say it is impossible of execution.

We say "I do not understand" of the natural world cheerfully, and endeavor to better ourselves and call it "science."

To be dismissive of "natural" evidence is called "ignorance." To dismiss the divine is called "sophistication."

וְאַתָּה תְּצַוֶּה אֶת־בְּנֵי יִשְׂרָאֵל וְיִקְחוּ אֵלֶיךָ שֶׁמֶן זַיִת זָךְ
כָּתִית לַמָּאוֹר לְהַעֲלֹת נֵר תָּמִיד: בְּאֹהֶל מוֹעֵד מִחוּץ
לַפָּרֹכֶת אֲשֶׁר עַל־הָעֵדֻת יַעֲרֹךְ אֹתוֹ אַהֲרֹן וּבָנָיו מֵעֶרֶב
עַד־בֹּקֶר לִפְנֵי יְהֹוָה   חֻקַּת עוֹלָם לְדֹרֹתָם מֵאֵת בְּנֵי
יִשְׂרָאֵל:

You shall command the children of Israel to bring you the clear oil of beaten olives for lighting, for making a flame to continually ascend. From evening to morning before God, Aaron and his sons shall arrange it in the tent of meeting, outside the curtain which is over the pact—an eternal ordinance, throughout their generations from the children of Israel.

Why can't they just use high-grade virgin olive oil? What's the big deal with grinding and beating the olives? It's because you just can't get the real clear and pure stuff until they pound the hell out of it (or you).

We have a classic rabbinic teaching drawn from Psalm 51:19: "The offering to God is a contrite spirit. . . ." The rabbis teach that the ultimate sacrifice is our smug expectation that we can do it alone, that we are in control of our own destiny. Suffering reminds us that we are not and, in so doing, purifies us. The teaching is not asceticism, nor offered as apologia or theodicy for the "thousand natural shocks flesh is heir to," but as a statement about the human condition. Anguish is simply a necessary precondition for the purification of the fuel (read: consciousness) required for the Tabernacle. To be sure, it is of little comfort to the bereaved and the price is never worth it. But the learning is sacred. Indeed, we are only broken if we refuse to teach others what we have learned, if we refuse to share the intense purity of the light in which we now behold life. The fuel for *this* light is purified by whatever is the opposite of arrogance.

Obviously, that cannot continue which is not being renewed, or, to put it differently, that which does not take into account the operation of time accelerates its own disappearance.

The adamant pillar, of whatever height or construction, must eventually decay. The zeal of its devotees, adherents, or servitors changes or warps or diminishes in direct proportion to the decay of the original object or proposition.

As the inevitable, human imperfection of the original grows increasingly more evident, greater prodigies of circumlocution, explanation, or hypocrisy are required of the worshippers. We Jews do not propitiate the monolith. We are renewed through the performance and repetition of simple acts: Fill the lamp, the oil will be consumed, fill the lamp again; obey the *mitzvot*, you will find yourself wanting, begin again.

21. EXODUS 33:20–23 / KI TISA

וַיֹּאמֶר לֹא תוּכַל לִרְאֹת אֶת־פָּנָי כִּי לֹא־יִרְאַנִי הָאָדָם
וָחָי: וַיֹּאמֶר יְדֹוָד הִנֵּה מָקוֹם אִתִּי וְנִצַּבְתָּ עַל־הַצּוּר:
וְהָיָה בַּעֲבֹר כְּבֹדִי וְשַׂמְתִּיךָ בְּנִקְרַת הַצּוּר וְשַׂכֹּתִי כַפִּי
עָלֶיךָ עַד־עָבְרִי: וַהֲסִרֹתִי אֶת־כַּפִּי וְרָאִיתָ אֶת־אֲחֹרָי
וּפָנַי לֹא יֵרָאוּ:

nd God said, "You cannot see My face, for a
person may not see Me and live." And God
said, "See, there is a place near Me. Station
yourself on the rock and, as My Presence passes by, I will
put you in a cleft of the rock and cover you with My hand
until I have passed by. Then I will remove My hand and
you will see My back; but My face may not be seen."

A t first reading, you might think that God, whose face cannot be seen, indeed has both a face and a back. Yet not only is anthropomorphism forbidden, but here it distracts us from the real teaching of the text. The Hebrew word for "My back" is *achorai*. In Hebrew it connotes not so much something spatial as temporal. God says to Moses, "You can see My afterward."

You can see what it's like *just after* I've been there. But you cannot see what it's like *while* I'm there, for that would mean that there was a part of you telling the rest of you that it was you who was there, and that would mean that not all of you was there, and if not all of you was there, then you couldn't possibly *be in the presence* of God.

M oses entreats God, "Let me see your honor" or "your glory."

God responds, "All of my goodness I will cause to pass before you."

The response is fitted to the understanding of the questioner.

God specifically states that no man can encompass all of God's presence and live. God will show only God's goodness; that which humankind could not possibly conceive as goodness—God's greater plan, the insignificance of man, the necessity of suffering, the likelihood of anguish, impermanence, loss, evanescence—these, as an ineluctable portion of God, are withheld.

The loving parent responds to the distraught child's "Tell me everything will be all right" not as a request for information, but as a plea for comfort. God has no face.

וְלֹא־יָכֹל מֹשֶׁה לָבוֹא אֶל־אֹהֶל מוֹעֵד כִּי־שָׁכַן עָלָיו
הֶעָנָן וּכְבוֹד יְדֹוָד מָלֵא אֶת־הַמִּשְׁכָּן: וּבְהֵעָלוֹת הֶעָנָן
מֵעַל הַמִּשְׁכָּן יִסְעוּ בְּנֵי יִשְׂרָאֵל בְּכֹל מַסְעֵיהֶם:
וְאִם־לֹא יֵעָלֶה הֶעָנָן וְלֹא יִסְעוּ עַד־יוֹם הֵעָלֹתוֹ: כִּי עֲנַן
יְדֹוָד עַל־הַמִּשְׁכָּן יוֹמָם וְאֵשׁ תִּהְיֶה לַיְלָה בּוֹ לְעֵינֵי
כָל־בֵּית־יִשְׂרָאֵל בְּכָל־מַסְעֵיהֶם:

A nd Moses was unable to enter the tent of meeting whenever the cloud of God's presence rested on it and filled the tabernacle. When the cloud lifted from the tabernacle, the children of Israel set out on all their journeys. But if the cloud did not lift, they did not journey. For the cloud of God's presence was on the tabernacle by day and there was fire on it at night in the sight of all the entire household of Israel throughout all their journeys.

LK

The wilderness Tabernacle—that Jerusalem Temple projected back hundreds of years into the desert—is also a mechanism for reconciliation. All that money plundered from the Egyptians only burnt a hole in the pockets of Israel. And first chance they got, it wound up in a golden calf. That must have been when God figured out that the children of Israel were only of *this* world and needed something tangible, something more constructive to do with their *gelt.* And now, with this calf-idol on their conscience, they were also more than a little ashamed. They needed some physical instrument through which they could absolve their guilt. So God told them to go and build a tabernacle—you know, a place where they could practice what has come to be known as organized religion. You might say that religion is a sanitized idol through which theophany might continue.

According to the great twentieth-century Italian Bible commentator Umberto Cassuto: "The Tabernacle is a kind of miniature Sinai, which can be transported from place to place, in order to accompany the children of Israel. . . ." (484) Our houses of worship even today are just little Sinais. We keep hoping against hope that one day we'll see a cloud or fire above, signaling that someone's home again.

But is there something in the notion that Moses could not enter the Tent of Meeting because the cloud rested on *him?*—that Moses could serve God when in his quality of *servant.* But when he was filled with the Holy Spirit—even though he may personally have been in direct communion with the Divine—to the Jewish people he was quite literally "good for nothing."

LEVITICUS / *VAYIKRA*

וַיִּקְרָא אֶל־מֹשֶׁה וַיְדַבֵּר יְדֹוָד אֵלָיו מֵאֹהֶל מוֹעֵד
לֵאמֹר: דַּבֵּר אֶל־בְּנֵי יִשְׂרָאֵל וְאָמַרְתָּ אֲלֵהֶם אָדָם
כִּי־יַקְרִיב מִכֶּם קָרְבָּן לַיְדֹוָד מִן־הַבְּהֵמָה מִן־הַבָּקָר
וּמִן־הַצֹּאן תַּקְרִיבוּ אֶת־קָרְבַּנְכֶם: אִם־עֹלָה קָרְבָּנוֹ
מִן־הַבָּקָר זָכָר תָּמִים יַקְרִיבֶנּוּ אֶל־פֶּתַח אֹהֶל מוֹעֵד
יַקְרִיב אֹתוֹ לִרְצֹנוֹ לִפְנֵי יְדֹוָד : וְסָמַךְ יָדוֹ עַל רֹאשׁ
הָעֹלָה וְנִרְצָה לוֹ לְכַפֵּר עָלָיו:

God called to Moses and spoke to him from the
tent of meeting saying: "Speak to the children of
Israel and say to them: 'When one of you offers
a sacrifice to God, you shall choose it from the cattle, the
herd, or the flock. If your offering is a burnt offering from
the herd, you shall make your offering a male without
blemish. You shall bring it to the entrance of the tent of
meeting, for acceptance in your behalf before God. You
shall place your hand on the head of the burnt offering so
that it will be acceptable on your behalf, to make atonement for you.' "

In the delicatessen, taped to the underside of the glass case that supports the cash register, right there above the *halvah*, breath mints, and antacids, is a dollar bill. Mysteriously rolled into that first dollar bill earned by this restaurant is the potential for all future profit. It's the same way with tomatoes in the garden also. The first one carries the regenerative potential for the species. Only a fool would squander that one. And so with the first issue of any womb. It must actually or (at least) symbolically be returned to the One who gave it, or entirely consumed during a sacral meal. Sacrifice is thus not so much a giving-up but a deal struck with the source of all life, a propitiation, if you will. After a while, centuries, it's no longer the first of the species—anyone will do—but the idea is the same. And then over the generations, as the ritual ossifies—just an annual donation to the priesthood to keep the whole thing going.

DM

The animal here described is certainly a priest manqué—a male without blemish, upon which hands are laid so that it is acceptable.

The urge to offer—or the memory of offering—human sacrifice, persists to this day. Every "Walk For . . ." is both a depiction and an attenuated performance of human sacrifice. The sacrificial practices of antique times may seem absurd, but they are no less prevalent today. The lottery ticket is a sacrifice, and our presidential campaigns and their attendant scandals and confessions are a ritualized purification-prior-to-slaughter, the impossible pomp and aggravated ceremony of presidential security revealing the buried truth that, mythologically, the candidate (without blemish) is being curried in order to be killed.

וְהָאֵשׁ עַל־הַמִּזְבֵּחַ תּוּקַד־בּוֹ לֹא תִכְבֶּה וּבִעֵר עָלֶיהָ
הַכֹּהֵן עֵצִים בַּבֹּקֶר בַּבֹּקֶר וְעָרַךְ עָלֶיהָ הָעֹלָה וְהִקְטִיר
עָלֶיהָ חֶלְבֵי הַשְּׁלָמִים: אֵשׁ תָּמִיד תּוּקַד עַל־הַמִּזְבֵּחַ לֹא
תִכְבֶּה:

The fire on the altar shall be kept burning by it, not
to go out: every morning the priest shall place
wood on it, arrange the burnt offering on it, and
turn the fat parts of the offerings of well-being into incense.
A perpetual fire shall be kept burning on the altar, not to be
extinguished.

LK

W hy is it so important to keep the fire burning on the altar? If it goes out, you light another one. Perhaps the fire is more than combustion; it resembles God. "The Lord your God is a consuming fire" (Deuteronomy 4:24; 9:3). And that might be why God twice instructs Moses and Aaron to make fires that must always burn: "Have the Israelites bring the clear oil of beaten olives for lighting, for kindling a perpetual flame" (Exodus 27:20; Leviticus 24:2). And now we learn that there is also supposed to be a perpetual fire going on the altar—a fire for consuming sacrifices and with them, the designs of men. Surely if they get consumed, then the request has been accepted (consummated?). Fire is the core symbol of transformation, the process whereby matter becomes energy, right before our eyes. Remember, the possibility of being consumed is ever present. It takes any "somethingnesss" and turns it into "nothingness."

DM

W e could say of the sacrifices, "How odd," or "superstitious"—but how much of modern life is blind, pleading propitiation of those we elect temporal intercessors with the divine: we pray to the investment counselor to turn our earned wealth into luxury; to the doctor to reverse the decree of mortality; to the lawyer to recast the die of human nature.

We moderns differ from the ancients not in the degree of our superstitious awe and fear, but in the identification of its source and in our choice of tactics. They sacrificed in thanks, or shame, or piety to an all-powerful God; we sacrifice in a deluded attempt at repression of our knowledge of our own insignificance.

אֶת־זֶה תֹּאכְלוּ מִכֹּל אֲשֶׁר בַּמָּיִם כֹּל אֲשֶׁר־לוֹ סְנַפִּיר
וְקַשְׂקֶשֶׂת בַּמַּיִם בַּיַּמִּים וּבַנְּחָלִים אֹתָם תֹּאכֵלוּ: וְכֹל
אֲשֶׁר אֵין־לוֹ סְנַפִּיר וְקַשְׂקֶשֶׂת בַּיַּמִּים וּבַנְּחָלִים מִכֹּל
שֶׁרֶץ הַמַּיִם וּמִכֹּל נֶפֶשׁ הַחַיָּה אֲשֶׁר בַּמָּיִם שֶׁקֶץ הֵם
לָכֶם:

Of everything that lives in water, this you
may eat: anything in water, whether in the seas
or rivers, that has fins and scales—these you
may eat. But anything in the seas or rivers that does not
have fins and scales, among all the swarming things of the
water and among all the other living creatures that are in
the water—they are an abomination for you.

LK

In other words, fish are okay, but anything else that doesn't appear by its very physiology to be "naturally" of the sea or the stream is forbidden. The whole idea seems to be that we too must learn to be naturally of this world and that we accomplish this by restricting our diets to food that is natural to its world. You eat weird stuff—creatures that do not fit naturally into their environments, then you too will cease to feel at home in your world. Will this food take me home?

DM

Why are there lawyers? To clarify that which is unclear in human dealings and to obfuscate that which is evident. This *parasha* seems to have been written by someone who was, or had had dealings with, a lawyer. If they have A and B, you may eat them. If they do not have both A and B, they are an abomination, and so they shall remain. And you may not eat them and shall hold them abhorrent. But, as with any law, the "ironclad" language of the injunction is an invitation to the adventurous mind, which gives us both the casuist and the artist, and the very clarity of the passage is a sort of index of despair.

וְלָקַח לְחַטֵּא אֶת־הַבַּיִת שְׁתֵּי צִפֳּרִים וְעֵץ אֶרֶז וּשְׁנִי
תוֹלַעַת וְאֵזֹב: וְשָׁחַט אֶת־הַצִּפֹּר הָאֶחָת אֶל־כְּלִי־חֶרֶשׂ
עַל־מַיִם חַיִּים: וְלָקַח אֶת־עֵץ־הָאֶרֶז וְאֶת־הָאֵזֹב וְאֵת
שְׁנִי הַתּוֹלַעַת וְאֵת הַצִּפֹּר הַחַיָּה וְטָבַל אֹתָם בְּדַם
הַצִּפֹּר הַשְּׁחוּטָה וּבַמַּיִם הַחַיִּים וְהִזָּה אֶל־הַבַּיִת שֶׁבַע
פְּעָמִים: וְחִטֵּא אֶת־הַבַּיִת בְּדַם הַצִּפּוֹר וּבַמַּיִם הַחַיִּים
וּבַצִּפֹּר הַחַיָּה וּבְעֵץ הָאֶרֶז וּבָאֵזֹב וּבִשְׁנִי הַתּוֹלָעַת:
וְשִׁלַּח אֶת־הַצִּפֹּר הַחַיָּה אֶל־מִחוּץ לָעִיר אֶל־פְּנֵי הַשָּׂדֶה
וְכִפֶּר עַל־הַבַּיִת וְטָהֵר:

To remove the sin of the house, he shall take two
birds, cedar wood, crimson yarn, and hyssop.
He shall slaughter the one bird over living water
in an earthen vessel. He shall take the cedar wood, the hyssop, the crimson yarn, and the live bird, and dip them in
the blood of the slaughtered bird and the living water, and
sprinkle on the house seven times. Having purged the houses with the blood of the bird, the fresh water, the live bird,
the cedar wood, the hyssop, and the crimson yarn, he shall
free the live bird outside the city in the open field. And he
shall make atonement for the house and it shall be ritually
purified.

LK

We seem to have lost the ability to discern the difference between being in a state of ritual purity and being in one of ritual defilement. Indeed, we have even forgotten that defilement comes from contact with death. But the categories are still there. All we have to show for our sophisticated amnesia is a nagging sense of discomfort and contamination. The Bible is, of course, keenly aware of these modes of being and here prescribes a ritual for returning to a state of purity from the inevitable contamination to which we are all condemned. It grows on the walls of our bedrooms like mold, and in the interiors of our psyches, an alien growth. It's immune to cleansers and medicines because it is not evil, dirt, or illness. But it's still there. Isn't that what organized religion is supposed to do? With water and blood and birds, hyssop and cedarwood and sacrifice (or whatever)—to make our houses fit again for habitation.

DM

How do we cleanse the unclean? How do we control the destructive? Adin Steinsaltz, the great contemporary Talmudist, says that it is a mistake to suppose that one can live a life without strife; it is ours only to decide on what level we wish to strive.

Freud wrote that it is not the purpose of psychoanalysis to produce happiness, but, rather, to bring the individual to a supportable level of misery. All ritual and all art must stem, originally, from the spontaneous individual impulse to reconcile the irreconcilable.

Love necessitates sorrow, as life necessitates death. One can wish away love, but this only creates a different sorrow—and the attendant necessity for support of the false idea of exemption.

Heschel writes that the Jews are the embodiment of conscience.

This troubling Jewish idea—our refusal to personify God—historically awakens discomfort and, periodically, rage, among non-Jews. Jewish willingness, indeed *determination*, to deal with the human as a way of making it holy, is, historically, seen by non-Jews as error.

But, as we humans are not God, nor even potentially godlike, the human must be periodically, inevitably, unclean.

The *thought* may be disturbing, but its acknowledgment is the first necessary step toward integration.

וַיְדַבֵּר יְדֹוָד אֶל־מֹשֶׁה לֵּאמֹר: דַּבֵּר אֶל־כָּל־עֲדַת
בְּנֵי־יִשְׂרָאֵל וְאָמַרְתָּ אֲלֵהֶם קְדֹשִׁים תִּהְיוּ כִּי קָדוֹשׁ אֲנִי
יְדֹוָד אֱלֹהֵיכֶם:

A nd God spoke to Moses, saying, "Speak to the
entire congregation of the children of Israel and
say to them, 'You shall be holy because I the
Lord your God am holy.' "

Holiness is being aware that you are in the presence of God. That something else is happening, something numinous, transcendent, other. Something that partakes of life and death, good and evil (remember the two trees in the Garden of Eden). An object, a place, a time, a person, is holy because it evokes the presence of God. We cover our heads, remove our shoes, look away in reverence. Unlike some spiritual traditions that see the world divided ontologically and irretrievably into sacred and profane, here we are told that, by our actions, we can realize the holiness in everything. In the words of Isaiah 6:3, "The fullness of all being is the presence of God."

What more appropriate overarching principle could there be than for God to tell us that we ourselves must act in such a way so as to remind one another of the presence of God. God says in effect: You should do this because I do it too! If I, God, can pull it off, then so can you. Indeed, (apparently) that's the main thing I do.

DM

The usual formula, *Dabaer el b'nai Yisrael* (Speak to the children of Israel), is here intensified by the insertion of *kol adat* (the entire congregation of), which, in conjunction with the future tense, *t'hiyu* (you shall be) would seem to leave no doubt that *each will be* holy. If any individual doubts the redemption of the multitude or of the objectionable, the provenance of this statement, unlikely as any ever made, reminds him that not only is HaShem all-powerful to save, but all-powerful to prognosticate.

The self-content Jew might say, "I know *I* might be holy, but the *Levys*, the *Horowitzes?*

Reference to this text might yield the answer "Yes, indeed, and perhaps you could look to *yourself.*"

לְמַעַן יֵדְעוּ דֹרֹתֵיכֶם כִּי בַסֻּכּוֹת הוֹשַׁבְתִּי אֶת־בְּנֵי
יִשְׂרָאֵל בְּהוֹצִיאִי אוֹתָם מֵאֶרֶץ מִצְרָיִם אֲנִי יְדֹוָד
אֱלֹקֵיכֶם: וַיְדַבֵּר מֹשֶׁה אֶת־מֹעֲדֵי יְדֹוָד אֶל־בְּנֵי יִשְׂרָאֵל:

I n order that your generations will know that I made the children of Israel dwell in booths when I brought them out of the land of Egypt, I the Lord am your God." So Moses declared to the children of Israel the set times of God.

LK

When God brought us out of Egypt, God made us dwell in these little shade booths in the desert. That's an odd pair, the paradigm redemption, the splitting of the sea, the biggest miracle of all time and making us dwell in flimsy little harvest booths—in the desert, made from what? Rocks?

The festivals of Passover and Sukkot are both seven days long, begin in the middle of their respective lunar months (that is, at the full moon), and are exactly six months apart. For one, the miracle is inescapable; for the other, there simply is no miracle. Go build your own booth. Manufacture your own salvation. I got it started, now you keep it going.

Just this is how you will reckon the days of the year, perpetually alternating between divine intervention and human workmanship.

DM

We are commanded to dwell in booths not because our ancestors did so, but because HaShem *caused them* to do so—the verse is not an invitation to empathy but a stern suggestion of submission to authority.

וַיְדַבֵּר יְדֹוָד אֶל־מֹשֶׁה בְּהַר סִינַי לֵאמֹר׃ דַּבֵּר אֶל־בְּנֵי
יִשְׂרָאֵל וְאָמַרְתָּ אֲלֵהֶם כִּי תָבֹאוּ אֶל־הָאָרֶץ אֲשֶׁר אֲנִי
נֹתֵן לָכֶם וְשָׁבְתָה הָאָרֶץ שַׁבָּת לַיְדֹוָד׃ שֵׁשׁ שָׁנִים
תִּזְרַע שָׂדֶךָ וְשֵׁשׁ שָׁנִים תִּזְמֹר כַּרְמֶךָ וְאָסַפְתָּ
אֶת־תְּבוּאָתָהּ׃ וּבַשָּׁנָה הַשְּׁבִיעִת שַׁבַּת שַׁבָּתוֹן יִהְיֶה
לָאָרֶץ שַׁבָּת לַיְדֹוָד שָׂדְךָ לֹא תִזְרָע וְכַרְמְךָ לֹא תִזְמֹר׃
אֵת סְפִיחַ קְצִירְךָ לֹא תִקְצוֹר וְאֶת־עִנְּבֵי נְזִירֶךָ לֹא
תִבְצֹר שְׁנַת שַׁבָּתוֹן יִהְיֶה לָאָרֶץ׃

G od spoke to Moses on Mount Sinai saying:
"Speak to the children of Israel and say to them:
'When you enter the land that I am giving to
you, the land shall observe a Sabbath of God. Six years
you may sow your field and six years you may prune
your vineyard and gather in its usufruct. But in the
seventh year the land shall have a Sabbath of complete
rest, a Sabbath of God. You shall neither sow your field
nor prune your vineyard. You shall neither reap the after-
growth of your harvest nor gather the grapes of your
untrimmed vines: It shall be a year of complete rest for the
land.' "

LK

What does the Sabbatical year have to do with Mount Sinai? The vast majority of the Torah's other paragraphs simply commence, "And God spoke to Moses. . . ." But this one—which goes on to give the details of the sabbatical year—adds the obvious location, "on Mount Sinai." Everything was told by God to Moses on Mount Sinai—why specify here the Sabbatical year?

According to the thirteenth-century Kabbalistic text *Sefer haTemunah*, a sabbatical year refers not to a year of fallow, but to a seven-thousand-year aeon. Our present universe is but one in a sequence of such sabbatical aeons. And, at the conclusion of the seven-times-seven sequence, they will all culminate in a fifty-thousand-year jubilee, when the whole of Creation returns to the womb—named *teshuva* or, according to later Kabbalists, nothingness.

Each universe is constructed according to a different dimension of God. First there was an aeon built on unrestricted loving. Following our present universe, there will be one assembled from mercy and forgiveness. In each universe, the Torah itself only makes sense according to the mode of its present aeon. Now, alas, we are in a universe of strict judgment. Our world and our Torah are cluttered with prohibitions, restrictions, and punishments.

In other words, of all the things God gave Moses, *on Mount Sinai,* God gave the possibility of refracting Torah itself through one seven-thousand-year-long lens after another.

DM

W hen you come into the land, the land will rest."
Perhaps, in addition to being a commandment, this is a description of a natural process, recognition of which might bring peace.

Children playing spontaneously create quarrels, to allow them a mechanism of rest; the cause of a bust is a boom; pride goeth before a fall; and we have all observed, and most have performed the modern demidrama of the overburdened individual, incapable of a conscious limitation of his activities, falling magically ill.

"If all Israel would observe the Sabbath, the *Moshiah* would come" might be understood to say that It is beyond the strength of Reason to confront Idolatry, one cannot "work harder" or, in the contemporary abomination, "work harder on oneself," to obtain peace. Which brings one back to the commandment.

NUMBERS / *BAMIDBAR*

שְׂאוּ אֶת־רֹאשׁ כָּל־עֲדַת בְּנֵי־יִשְׂרָאֵל לְמִשְׁפְּחֹתָם לְבֵית אֲבֹתָם בְּמִסְפַּר שֵׁמוֹת כָּל־זָכָר לְגֻלְגְּלֹתָם:

Take a census of the whole Israelite community by the clans of its tribes, listing the names, every male, head by head.

There used to be a TV show when I was growing up called *Naked City.* They showed an aerial view of Manhattan, played some weird music, and then the announcer said something like "There are nine million stories in the naked city and tonight we'll tell you one of them."

This reminds me of what it is like for me to be the rabbi of a congregation. I sit up there on that stage at the front of the prayer hall and watch everyone assemble for the High Holy Days. One by one, they walk into the room—families with new babies, families where there will be an empty seat, old friends reuniting, enemies trying to avoid one another, enemies asking forgiveness, someone who's been told by his doctor that this will be his last Rosh Hashanah, you know—the whole circus. And they know one or two about you.

So what I'm saying is that after you've been the rabbi for as long as I have, you know a story or two about each person out there: something joyous, something shameful, a hope, a death, a secret wish. That's simply what it means to take a census of the community and that's what it also means to be in a community.

Much of the tropism to war must be infant sacrifice. The English and Germans—armies of the two most advanced and philosophic countries in the world of 1914—convened across a trench to slaughter each other. Sixty thousand young men were sent to Vietnam to die in an action pointless and absurd unless its point was the very death of these young men. They died to assuage anxiety on the part of their elders—anxiety over the place of America or of the elders themselves, in the world. Or, to put it differently, they died as a sacrifice to the sun god—a propitiation. The student opposition to the war was disproportionately Jewish—that is to say, Jews were less likely to embrace blindly the tropism to infant sacrifice. Can one trace the roots of that reluctance to the *Akedah,* and see the autonomic attempt at its reinstitution, in this story of the draft? Does a nation require a draft as much for its psychic integrity as for its military purposes? Was the draft a proclamation of having as a nation succeeded to the status of Elder; and, so, of being prepared to sacrifice the young?

וַיְדַבֵּר יְדֹוָד אֶל־מֹשֶׁה לֵּאמֹר: דַּבֵּר אֶל־אַהֲרֹן וְאֶל־בָּנָיו
לֵאמֹר כֹּה תְבָרְכוּ אֶת־בְּנֵי יִשְׂרָאֵל אָמוֹר לָהֶם: יְבָרֶכְךָ
יְדֹוָד וְיִשְׁמְרֶךָ: יָאֵר יְדֹוָד פָּנָיו אֵלֶיךָ וִיחֻנֶּךָּ: יִשָּׂא יְדֹוָד
פָּנָיו אֵלֶיךָ וְיָשֵׂם לְךָ שָׁלוֹם: וְשָׂמוּ אֶת־שְׁמִי עַל־בְּנֵי
יִשְׂרָאֵל וַאֲנִי אֲבָרֲכֵם:

God spoke to Moses saying: "Speak to Aaron and
his sons saying: 'Thus you shall bless the children of Israel.' "Say to them:

May God bless you and protect you.
May God let the light of God's presence shine on you
and be gracious to you.
May God look kindly upon you and grant you
peace!

Thus they shall set My name upon the children of
Israel and I will bless them."

The priestly blessing is composed of three verses; each one has two parts. May God do this and may God do that. One tradition suggests that the first clause is causally connected to the second, in the language of symbolic logic, they are "If-then" clauses. If God blesses you, then you will be protected. If God deals kindly with you, then you will be dealt with graciously. And, if God bestows favor on you, then you will be granted peace.

But this only raises the obvious question: If that's the goal, why not then just ask for the blessings in the second clause to begin with? Perhaps it is because you can ask for blessing, kindness, and favor but not for protection, grace, and peace—they are something else. Not even the high priest can coax those out of God. They are beyond asking even though they may be the reason for the request!

T*hus* shall you bless the children of Israel . . ."
    You will bless them by *speaking* to them, for the priestly blessing is not a *wish*—"*May* the Lord . . ."—but a *description*—"The Lord *will* . . ."

The verses are the description of a contract, or of the natural progress of a natural relationship. God says: "When you [the priests] relate to Israel its good fortune, they *will* identify themselves as My own."

וְהָאסַפְסֻף אֲשֶׁר בְּקִרְבּוֹ הִתְאַוּוּ תַּאֲוָה וַיָּשֻׁבוּ וַיִּבְכּוּ
גַּם בְּנֵי יִשְׂרָאֵל וַיֹּאמְרוּ מִי יַאֲכִלֵנוּ בָּשָׂר: זָכַרְנוּ
אֶת־הַדָּגָה אֲשֶׁר־נֹאכַל בְּמִצְרַיִם חִנָּם אֵת הַקִּשֻּׁאִים
וְאֵת הָאֲבַטִּחִים וְאֶת־הֶחָצִיר וְאֶת־הַבְּצָלִים
וְאֶת־הַשּׁוּמִים: וְעַתָּה נַפְשֵׁנוּ יְבֵשָׁה אֵין כֹּל בִּלְתִּי
אֶל־הַמָּן עֵינֵינוּ:

The riffraff in its midst had a great craving and reversed everything. And the children of Israel wept and said, "If only we had meat to eat! We remember the fish that we used to eat free in Egypt, the cucumbers, the melons, the leeks, the onions, and the garlic. Now our souls are shriveled. There is nothing at all to look at except this manna!"

But manna was the ultimate delicacy! According to midrashic accounts, the stuff was magical; it tasted like anything you were in the mood for. So why on earth would someone want to trade such nectar of the God for "fish, cucumbers, melons, leeks, onions, and garlic"?

That is a funny list. No bread, no wine, no milk, no honey. But maybe it's not supposed to describe a well-balanced diet. Except for the melons (and maybe the cucumbers), the menu is lopsided toward the salty, spicy, and fishy. And yet the grumblers grumbled that back in Egypt this particularly savory menu was all for free.

We have several traditions suggesting that the experience of Egyptian slavery was not without its pleasures. As long as the Israelites made each day's quota of bricks, their taskmasters didn't much care what they did. Indeed, their taskmasters probably even encouraged licentiousness and promiscuity. What better a way to deter revolutionary fantasies? But now, in exchange for their freedom, they realize that they have also traded away all this free sex for sexual proscription, religious law, and guilt. It's not their gullets that are shriveled! No wonder they want to go back! Wouldn't you?

J am Today"

William Dean Howells wrote, "He was old enough to realize that no one is less happy than a successful man."

Rabbi Art Green teaches that *"eyeh asher eyeh"*—"I will be what I will be"—in addition to being a proclamation, can also be understood as a promise; i.e., I will always fascinate, I will never cease to draw you on (*Ein Sof*)—one of the names of God: "without end."

How supremely fortunate the individual who has found perennial, elusive, life-giving mystery—in a professional pursuit, a mate, the Torah (which the rabbis likened to "a wife with a narrow womb").

It has been said, "A poem is never completed— only abandoned"; and perhaps God's denial to Moses of entrance into the Promised Land was a final act of favor. He died, as he lived, with a goal, which sustained, which never failed to fascinate. He knew hardship, and disillusion, but he never knew regret.

וַיַּ֣הַס כָּלֵ֔ב אֶת־הָעָ֖ם אֶל־מֹשֶׁ֑ה וַיֹּ֗אמֶר עָלֹ֤ה נַעֲלֶה֙
וְיָרַ֣שְׁנוּ אֹתָ֔הּ כִּֽי־יָכ֥וֹל נוּכַ֖ל לָֽהּ׃ וְהָ֣אֲנָשִׁ֗ים אֲשֶׁר־
עָל֤וּ עִמּוֹ֙ אָֽמְר֔וּ לֹ֥א נוּכַ֖ל לַעֲל֣וֹת אֶל־הָעָ֑ם כִּֽי־חָזָ֥ק ה֖וּא
מִמֶּֽנּוּ׃ וַיֹּצִ֜יאוּ דִּבַּ֤ת הָאָ֙רֶץ֙ אֲשֶׁ֣ר תָּר֣וּ אֹתָ֔הּ אֶל־בְּנֵ֥י
יִשְׂרָאֵ֖ל לֵאמֹ֑ר הָאָ֡רֶץ אֲשֶׁר֩ עָבַ֨רְנוּ בָ֜הּ לָת֣וּר אֹתָ֗הּ
אֶ֣רֶץ אֹכֶ֤לֶת יֽוֹשְׁבֶ֙יהָ֙ הִ֔וא וְכָל־הָעָ֛ם אֲשֶׁר־רָאִ֥ינוּ
בְתוֹכָ֖הּ אַנְשֵׁ֥י מִדּֽוֹת׃ וְשָׁ֣ם רָאִ֗ינוּ אֶת־הַנְּפִילִ֛ים בְּנֵ֥י
עֲנָ֖ק מִן־הַנְּפִלִ֑ים וַנְּהִ֤י בְעֵינֵ֙ינוּ֙ כַּֽחֲגָבִ֔ים וְכֵ֥ן הָיִ֖ינוּ
בְּעֵינֵיהֶֽם׃

A nd Caleb hushed the people before Moses and said, "We can do it. We can claim what's ours. We have what it takes." But the men who had gone up with him said, "There's no way we could ever go up against strength like theirs." Whereupon they began to circulate calumnies about the land they had just scouted, saying that it was a land that devoured its inhabitants and that all the people whom they saw there were huge. "We saw there the Nephilim, the descendants of Anak, giants! We felt like grasshoppers and we must have looked that way to them too!"

The *Nephilim*, these Goliaths who inhabit the Promised Land, are already mentioned back in Genesis 6:4. There we learn that in those primordial times "the *Nephilim* were then on earth." This account is so long ago, at the beginning of Genesis, because it is also deep within the childhood memory of every human being. Now *there* was a time when real giants prowled the land and we felt like grasshoppers. It is an indelible, if repressed, unconscious memory in each of us. Contrary to the intended effect of nursery pastel colors and soft lullabies, this was frequently not a time of abiding personal security. Who could relax with giants everywhere?

Taking possession of the Land of Canaan may therefore also be a metaphor for returning to the scene of one's childhood—now prepared to stand one's own against its inhabitants, to conquer it for oneself. It is going back to when you were a child among huge people. If you were lucky, they were kind and loving, but even if they were, the thought must have crossed every child's mind: If those guys ever get mad at me, I'm toast. So, to be able to stand toe-to-toe with them, now that you're grown up yourself, must surely be one of the great joys of coming of age.

Menahem Mendl Morgenstern of Kotzk says that it's all right to say you feel like a grasshopper in your own eyes—that means you're alert—but when you start guessing what you look like to someone else, you've given them permission to define you, so you're still a child. For this reason, Caleb, who refuses to let anyone else define him, is a man and, along with Joshua, was one of only two men of the wilderness generation to live to enter the Promised Land. But that's another story.

DM

Most of us, I believe, wonder how we would act if faced with the opportunity for heroism.

Here the Israelites suggest that, yes, there is a time for heroism, but that time is *surely* not when one is frightened—that any rational person would concur that the only possible response to the overwhelming is capitulation.

Hannah Arendt, in her *Eichmann in Jerusalem*, lists many instances of participants in the Final Solution who "were not Nazis in their hearts," people who, in their own estimation, "went along" *within* the organization in order to mitigate worse horrors than those in which they participated. These Nazis "with reservations" murdered—with a weapon or with a fiat—hundreds of thousands.

Arendt writes also that a dark secret of the Shoah was that mass murder of the Jews would have

113

been impossible without Jewish capitulation, and, in fact, aid.

Jewish organizations and individuals, working, of course, for a variety of reasons, assisted the Nazis in registration, "classification," and deportation of their fellow Jews. How terrible to be called to resist evil and to refuse, denominating such suggested resistance "unreasonable."

וַיִּקַּח קֹרַח בֶּן־יִצְהָר בֶּן־קְהָת בֶּן־לֵוִי וְדָתָן וַאֲבִירָם בְּנֵי
אֱלִיאָב וְאוֹן בֶּן־פֶּלֶת בְּנֵי רְאוּבֵן: וַיָּקֻמוּ לִפְנֵי מֹשֶׁה
וַאֲנָשִׁים מִבְּנֵי־יִשְׂרָאֵל חֲמִשִּׁים וּמָאתָיִם נְשִׂיאֵי עֵדָה
קְרִאֵי מוֹעֵד אַנְשֵׁי־שֵׁם: וַיִּקָּהֲלוּ עַל־מֹשֶׁה וְעַל־אַהֲרֹן
וַיֹּאמְרוּ אֲלֵהֶם רַב־לָכֶם כִּי כָל־הָעֵדָה כֻּלָּם קְדֹשִׁים
וּבְתוֹכָם יְהֹוָה וּמַדּוּעַ תִּתְנַשְּׂאוּ עַל־קְהַל יְהֹוָה :

N ow Korah, son of Izhar, son of Kohath, son of
Levi, took himself, along with Dathan and
Abiram, sons of Eliab, and On, son of Peleth—
descendants of Reuben—and rose up before Moses, along
with two hundred and fifty children of Israel, chieftains
of the community, chosen in the assembly, men of repute.
They assembled themselves against Moses and Aaron and
said to them, "You have made yourselves too important:
All the community are holy, all of them, and God is in
their midst. Why do you raise yourselves above God's
congregation?"

We know Korah is a bad guy. Our tip-off is when the earth opens its mouth and swallows him. The question is, what makes him deserving of such ignominy?

Moses and Korah represent mirror images of leadership. Like all good leaders, Moses respects the people and consistently shuns his office. (We recall that back at Sinai, after the business with the golden calf, when God wanted to destroy them all, Moses says, "Take me instead!" We cannot imagine Korah making the same offer.) Korah, on the other hand, only seems intoxicated with his own self-importance and what leadership will add to it. He hijacks Moses' constructive lie that "everyone is holy" for his own personal agenda. "If everyone is holy, then how come Moses gets to be the leader?"

Yaakov Yosef of Polnoye, a second-generation Hasidic master, in his *Toledot Yaakov Yosef*, takes it even further. Like so many of the Hasidic writers, he is especially interested in the seductions of religious leadership. Moses, he suggests, easily found fault in himself because those who are truly close to God, understand how imperfect they really are. Korah, in contrast, found fault in others and praised himself. Indeed, Korah accuses Moses of Korah's own sin: trying to arrogate power for himself. Moses' humility grows from his dependence on the community.

Korah's arrogance springs from his separation from it. The contest between Moses and Korah thus becomes an archetypical struggle.

Rabbinic tradition is fond of pointing out that the Hebrew *vayikakh*, "and he [Korah] betook himself" in Aramaic becomes *v'it-paleg*, "and Korah separated himself." Korah's sin was that he separated himself from the community and thereby threatened not only its unity but its survival. And so he himself was forcibly separated from the community: the earth swallowed him up.

DM

Most leaders are either idolized or resented. The human capacity for umbrage—not to say simple contrariness—is too great to admit mere simple, rational acceptance of hierarchy.

Rav lakhem, the Israelites say of Aaron and Moses—"You're too big for yourself." I think we can understand the phrase as antagonistic not only in content, but in form—a "street epithet."

Taunted and faced with mutiny, Moses is exasperated. He falls on his face, then composes himself and assaults the mob in its own language. *Rav lakhem* is here clearly understandable as "Oh *yeah?*" And he threatens them: "Bring your incense tomorrow and let's just see who is chosen of God."

I never liked Moses. I don't like his preferment, his power, his attitude. They all seem to me distinctly un-Jewish. I feel they indicate that he was most probably not a Jew at all but an Egyptian—an illegitimate son (compare Freud) of Pharaoh's daughter. And, so, no kin of mine.

Then it occurred to me that my reaction identified me absolutely as a Jew—as an opponent of authority, as headstrong, rebellious, arrogant, as everything Moses asserts against our people—and this understanding—this ancient, persistent description of the Jewish attitude—seemed to me to support the argument for divine inspiration and Mosaic authorship of the Torah.

וַיִּחַר־אַף אֱלֹקִים כִּי־הוֹלֵךְ הוּא וַיִּתְיַצֵּב מַלְאַךְ יְדֹוָד
בַּדֶּרֶךְ לְשָׂטָן לוֹ וְהוּא רֹכֵב עַל־אֲתֹנוֹ וּשְׁנֵי נְעָרָיו עִמּוֹ:
וַתֵּרֶא הָאָתוֹן אֶת־מַלְאַךְ יְדֹוָד נִצָּב בַּדֶּרֶךְ וְחַרְבּוֹ
שְׁלוּפָה בְּיָדוֹ וַתֵּט הָאָתוֹן מִן־הַדֶּרֶךְ וַתֵּלֶךְ בַּשָּׂדֶה וַיַּךְ
בִּלְעָם אֶת־הָאָתוֹן לְהַטֹּתָהּ הַדָּרֶךְ: וַיַּעֲמֹד מַלְאַךְ יְדֹוָד
בְּמִשְׁעוֹל הַכְּרָמִים גָּדֵר מִזֶּה וְגָדֵר מִזֶּה: וַתֵּרֶא הָאָתוֹן
אֶת־מַלְאַךְ יְדֹוָד וַתִּלָּחֵץ אֶל־הַקִּיר וַתִּלְחַץ אֶת־רֶגֶל
בִּלְעָם אֶל־הַקִּיר וַיֹּסֶף לְהַכֹּתָהּ: וַיּוֹסֶף מַלְאַךְ־יְדֹוָד
עֲבוֹר וַיַּעֲמֹד בְּמָקוֹם צָר אֲשֶׁר אֵין־דֶּרֶךְ לִנְטוֹת יָמִין
וּשְׂמֹאול: וַתֵּרֶא הָאָתוֹן אֶת־מַלְאַךְ יְדֹוָד וַתִּרְבַּץ תַּחַת
בִּלְעָם וַיִּחַר־אַף בִּלְעָם וַיַּךְ אֶת־הָאָתוֹן בַּמַּקֵּל: וַיִּפְתַּח
יְדֹוָד אֶת־פִּי הָאָתוֹן וַתֹּאמֶר לְבִלְעָם מֶה־עָשִׂיתִי לְךָ
כִּי הִכִּיתַנִי זֶה שָׁלֹשׁ רְגָלִים: וַיֹּאמֶר בִּלְעָם לָאָתוֹן כִּי
הִתְעַלַּלְתְּ בִּי לוּ יֶשׁ־חֶרֶב בְּיָדִי כִּי עַתָּה הֲרַגְתִּיךְ:

B ut God was angry that he [Bilaam] went, so a
messenger of the Lord stationed himself in the way
as an adversary against him. And he was riding on
his she-ass and his two servants were with him. And the
ass saw the messenger of the Lord standing in the way with
his sword in his hand, and the ass swerved from the road

and went into the field. Bilaam hit the ass to get it back on the path. And the messenger of the Lord stood in the vineyard path with a wall on either side. And the ass saw the messenger of the Lord, so she squeezed toward the wall and smashed Bilaam's foot against the wall. So he hit her again. And again the messenger of the Lord moved ahead and stood in a narrow place, so that this time there was no place to move either to the right or the left. So when the ass saw the messenger of the Lord, she lay down under Bilaam. Bilaam was furious and whacked the ass with his staff. Then the Lord opened the mouth of the she-ass, and she said to Bilaam, "What have I done to you that you should hit me these three times?" And Bilaam said to the ass, "How dare you mock me. If I had a sword, I'd kill you right here."

I have never been entirely satisfied with Franz Rosenzweig's famous reply to the skeptic who asked him if he believed that Bilaam's ass really talked. The great German philosopher thought for a while and answered with a wink, "On the *Shabbos* they read it from the Torah, I believe it."

With a similar trick, the rabbis explain that this talking she-ass (or, to be precise, its vocal mouth) was one of the minor miracles, exceptions to the natural order, set in motion by divine fiat on the eve of the sixth day of creation. Asses don't see angels or speak—except for Bilaam's—and that was foreordained since before the creation of the world. Case closed.

Taken literally, the whole story is obviously silly. Or is it? Even though it makes us uncomfortable, animals can and do know things hidden from human perception and people do routinely communicate with them.

The biblical author even warns us that we are reading a fable. There are three confrontations with the invisible messenger of the Lord, each one increasingly difficult to ignore. Even a dumb animal—and she-asses are notoriously dumb—can see that Bilaam's mission is contrary to God's plan, even though the great seer cannot. The question is, can this great seer *raise* himself to the level of a she-ass? Can we?

The habits and principles which sustain us are, in the main, unfortunately, drab and undramatic.

The Pilot's Law of Conservatism: "Where there is any doubt, there is not doubt"; the old rabbinical injunction: "If you must obey one law, let it be: 'Do not lie' "; in fact, even the dramatist's best rule: "If you suspect that perhaps you should cut, *cut*"—these do not inflame or inspire. On the contrary, they are the *antidote* to that inspiration which, too often and to our chagrin, is revealed as self-absorption, or idolatry.

The lowly ass has protected and sustained Bilaam, and, like many another good dull principle, is derided and discarded in the heat of sin from which we, inspired, conceive ourselves immune.

וַתִּקְרַבְנָה בְּנוֹת צְלָפְחָד בֶּן־חֵפֶר בֶּן־גִּלְעָד בֶּן־מָכִיר בֶּן־מְנַשֶּׁה לְמִשְׁפְּחֹת מְנַשֶּׁה בֶן־יוֹסֵף וְאֵלֶּה שְׁמוֹת בְּנֹתָיו מַחְלָה נֹעָה וְחָגְלָה וּמִלְכָּה וְתִרְצָה: וַתַּעֲמֹדְנָה לִפְנֵי מֹשֶׁה וְלִפְנֵי אֶלְעָזָר הַכֹּהֵן וְלִפְנֵי הַנְּשִׂיאִם וְכָל־הָעֵדָה פֶּתַח אֹהֶל־מוֹעֵד לֵאמֹר: אָבִינוּ מֵת בַּמִּדְבָּר וְהוּא לֹא־הָיָה בְּתוֹךְ הָעֵדָה הַנּוֹעָדִים עַל־יְהוָה בַּעֲדַת־קֹרַח כִּי־בְחֶטְאוֹ מֵת וּבָנִים לֹא־הָיוּ לוֹ: לָמָּה יִגָּרַע שֵׁם־אָבִינוּ מִתּוֹךְ מִשְׁפַּחְתּוֹ כִּי אֵין לוֹ בֵּן תְּנָה־לָּנוּ אֲחֻזָּה בְּתוֹךְ אֲחֵי אָבִינוּ:

T he daughters of Zelophehad of the family Manasseh—son of Hepher, son of Gilead, son of Machir, son of Manasseh, son of Joseph—came forward. These are the names of his daughters: Mahlah, Noa, Hoglah, Milcah, and Tirzah. They stood before Moses, Eleazar the priest, the chieftains, and the entire assembly, at the entrance of the Tent of meeting, and they said, "Our father died in the wilderness; and he was not one of the faction which assembled against God, Korah's faction. But he died for his own sin; he had no sons. Why should our father's name be lost to his clan just because he had no son? Give us an inheritance among our father's kin."

Why do they bother telling Moses that their father was not one of Korah's band of rebels? What possible difference could such information make?

Only this: By introducing Korah, we are invited to consider that the story of Zelophehad's daughters is not just some long-overdue good news for feminists (which it certainly is). The story is about political rebellion and challenges to Mosaic leadership. Like the story of Korah, the family lineage of the daughters begins the narrative. We are told whom they are and from whom they've come even before we are told what they want.

But these are not like Korah. "Our father was not part of Korah's group" (who were swallowed by the earth). "He was a man who died for his own reasons." (In the Hebrew Bible, death is never without a lesson.) "And we, his five daughters, are not a bunch of rebels either. We have what we believe is a legitimate complaint against the present regime and therefore we request a hearing." And, of course, unlike Korah and his band, their request is granted.

The Talmud is the only legal code that religiously records minority opinions.

nd Moses brought their case before God."
A postal worker is dismissed because her stride is one inch short of that mandated by regulations. Her service is excellent, her rounds are completed on time, but she is denounced for falling afoul of regulations and she is dismissed.

A family outside Chicago adopts a child at birth. When the child is four, the man who impregnated the birth mother successfully sues for custody—the child is wrenched from the only home it has ever known and given to a cruel stranger.

Appellate courts rule that a convicted man, sentenced to death, cannot be reprieved, even though incontrovertible new evidence shows him to be innocent. "Innocence," they say, "is no grounds for reversal."

Moses, also, is faced with an unprecedented situation. The daughters of Zelophehad are barred by law from inheriting. They appeal outside of the law, upon the simple human merits of the case.

Inherent in their plea is the understanding that codified law exists only as an attempt to provide justice and mercy; that, as a human construct, it must be imperfect; and that a system which does not allow final appeal (to that human impulse which gave rise to the code) is an abomination.

Himmler told the S.S. that history would record

their great achievement—that they had performed the atrocities ordered, and, yet, had managed to retain their essential decency.

Moses realized that he was unable, in conscience, to perform as ordered, and he brought his problem to God.

וַיְדַבֵּר יְהֹוָה אֶל־מֹשֶׁה לֵּאמֹר: דַּבֵּר אֶל־בְּנֵי יִשְׂרָאֵל
וְאָמַרְתָּ אֲלֵהֶם כִּי אַתֶּם עֹבְרִים אֶת־הַיַּרְדֵּן אַרְצָה
כְּנָעַן: וְהִקְרִיתֶם לָכֶם עָרִים עָרֵי מִקְלָט תִּהְיֶינָה לָכֶם
וְנָס שָׁמָּה רֹצֵחַ מַכֵּה־נֶפֶשׁ בִּשְׁגָגָה: וְהָיוּ לָכֶם הֶעָרִים
לְמִקְלָט מִגֹּאֵל וְלֹא יָמוּת הָרֹצֵחַ עַד־עָמְדוֹ לִפְנֵי הָעֵדָה
לַמִּשְׁפָּט: וְהֶעָרִים אֲשֶׁר תִּתֵּנוּ שֵׁשׁ־עָרֵי מִקְלָט תִּהְיֶינָה
לָכֶם: אֵת שְׁלֹשׁ הֶעָרִים תִּתְּנוּ מֵעֵבֶר לַיַּרְדֵּן וְאֵת שְׁלֹשׁ
הֶעָרִים תִּתְּנוּ בְּאֶרֶץ כְּנָעַן עָרֵי מִקְלָט תִּהְיֶינָה: לִבְנֵי
יִשְׂרָאֵל וְלַגֵּר וְלַתּוֹשָׁב בְּתוֹכָם תִּהְיֶינָה שֵׁשׁ־הֶעָרִים
הָאֵלֶּה לְמִקְלָט לָנוּס שָׁמָּה כָּל־מַכֵּה־נֶפֶשׁ בִּשְׁגָגָה:

And God spoke to Moses, saying: "Speak to the children of Israel and say to them: When you cross over the Jordan into the Land of Canaan, you shall designate for yourselves cities. They will be for you cities of refuge. There a manslayer who has unintentionally committed murder may flee. The cities shall be a sanctuary from the avenger of blood-guilt, so that the manslayer may not die unless he has stood trial before the community. The number of cities for you that you designate shall be six cities of refuge. Three shall be assigned beyond the Jordan, and three shall be assigned in the Land of Canaan; they shall be cities of refuge. These six cities shall serve the children of Israel as well as resident aliens among them for a sanctuary, so that someone who murders someone unintentionally may have a place to flee."

What brings *you* here, neighbor?"
The people who lived there, in one of those cities—what did they say when they wanted to strike up a conversation with a newcomer? Were they circumspect or brazen in their curiosity? And when they contemplated their own estates, were they paralyzed by guilt or just happy to be safe from the blood-avenging Mountie who always caught his man? (As a young rabbi, I once served as a prison chaplain at a maximum-security federal penitentiary in Ohio. I was astonished to discover that literally every single inmate sincerely believed he was innocent, incarcerated by some terrible mistake.)

What must it have been like to live in a city of refuge, this place of neither acquittal nor punishment? And what must it have done to even casual intercourse? Imagine: Every single person you'd meet, every single day, had accidentally murdered another human being. From the mayor to a panhandler: "My fellow citizens, I urge your support for this new bond initiative"; "Mister, can you spare a quarter for a cup of coffee?" They were all united by shame; they all had innocent blood on their hands. And there was no escape either. (Sure, everyone talked about taking a vacation, someday, but no one ever seemed to get around to leaving.)

Perhaps it was no different from life in any city, anywhere, anytime.

DM

As you are now passing the Jordan River toward the Land of Canaan." That is, you are undergoing a transition, and *as* you are maturing, you are required to perform an act of maturity.

The desire for blood revenge is so strong and irrational that it may not only supercede but nullify both reason and law (compare the Unwritten Law).

In America demagogues sell death, or, better, trade death for peace—they barter the death penalty for votes, pandering to and perverting the electorate.

Capital punishment is held, in most of the world, to be barbaric—it is irreversible, cruel, and degrading to those in whose name it is performed. It does not deter crime—its survival is owed to an immaturity on the part of the body politic and its exploitation by the corrupt.

In capital punishment, the state, the electorate, desire not to *punish* the killer, but to *emulate* him—to arrogate to themselves that horrible power taken by the murderer. (The psychological component of capital punishment operates hydraulically: in killing the murderer I supress [deny, extirpate] my own murderous impulses.)

The Torah invokes the ritual crossing over and abjures us not "to lay aside" our murderous impulses but to accept that, being human, we are prone to revert to savagery and so must create mechanisms to protect both the accused and the body politic from blood-rage when self-control—as it will—dissolves.

DEUTERONOMY / *DEVARIM*

38. DEUTERONOMY 1:12–13 / DEVARIM

אֵיכָה אֶשָּׂא לְבַדִּי טָרְחֲכֶם וּמַשַּׂאֲכֶם וְרִיבְכֶם: הָבוּ
לָכֶם אֲנָשִׁים חֲכָמִים וּנְבֹנִים וִידֻעִים לְשִׁבְטֵיכֶם
וַאֲשִׂימֵם בְּרָאשֵׁיכֶם:

How can I alone bear your troubles, your burdens, and your bickering! Bring people from your tribes who are wise, sage, and experienced, and I will appoint them as your heads.

Moses' relationship with the Jewish people has been anything but lovey-dovey. Like all leaders, he seems caught in a love-hate relationship with the flock. From the burning bush where Moses tells God to pick someone else, to his complaint that he is of impeded speech, Moses consistently resists the burden of leading the people. When he tells the Jews God will free them, they laugh at him, and at the first sight of the advancing Egyptian army, they sarcastically ask him if it was because there weren't enough graves in Egypt that he had to bring them out into the wilderness to die. By the time Moses gets up on Mount Sinai after the golden calf, he refers to the Jews as God's people but not his. Indeed, the only mention of any reciprocal emotion at all from the Jews toward their white-haired leader was that they cried a lot once he was dead. If anything, Moses would love to be out of the job and, apparently, a few times, rid of most of the people too. Rashi sees in the redundancy of "troubles, burdens, and bickering" further proof that they were not only obnoxious, but litigious as well.

The story is told of Rabbi Shmelke of Nikolsburg that when he served as rabbi in a community he would always hang his walking stick and his knapsack on the wall of the synagogue. If anyone is displeased with my judgments, he would say, I am prepared to leave at once.

Moses' father-in-law, Jethro, came up with a solution back in Exodus 18 and recounted here: Insulate the leader within a bureaucracy! This is more than the simple delegation of responsibility; it is the creation of artificial, ritual distance necessary for the leader to be able to lead and love.

DM

It is written in Deuteronomy 17:15, "The time will come when you will want to choose for yourself a king."

One wonders why. Why must it be inevitable that a people would wish to so burden itself?

The answer, I think, is here: that "HaShem has multiplied you, and behold you, today as numerous as the stars in the sky."

HaShem, we are told, will increase the Jews as per agreement. Verse 12 (beginning with the *vav*) can be translated as *"But,* how can I [Moses] bear, unaided, the trouble of you . . . ?"

The promised, wished-for expansion of the Jewish people, then, is not an unmixed blessing. It is inevitable that expansion will bring its own problems. Addressed here is the impossibility of Moses himself dealing with the judicial complaints of the increased multitude.

Longevity, prosperity, success, in short, bring their own attendant dilemmas (see, for instance, the State of Israel).

The small, harassed band is fiercely cohesive from necessity; the larger group desires leaders. Finally, when the group has grown so large as to prevent individual knowledge of its representatives, they demand and are burdened with a King—as in the American presidential race. Healthy increase becomes elaboration, which becomes abstraction, and abstraction progresses, inevitably, into absurdity.

Both the good idea (the Garden of Eden), and the bad idea (the Tower of Babel) are subject to the laws of entropy—all human endeavor and all human understanding are, essentially, as naught. What remains? The unknowable nature of HaShem, and the Torah.

39. DEUTERONOMY 6:4 /
V'ETHANAN

שְׁמַע יִשְׂרָאֵל יְדֹוָד אֱלֹקֵינוּ יְדֹוָד אֶחָד׃

ear, O Israel! The Lord is our God, the Lord one.

We once knew a great unity, when we were very young. Then, all being was one seamless, living organism. We were more than a part of it: we were *of* it and it was *of* us. Then we were born and everything began to fall apart, mothers and children, fathers and mothers, siblings, lovers, families, villages, nations. Earliest childhood is living in the unity; adulthood is surviving the brokenness. And what has come to be called spiritual maturity is remembering the ancient unity and trying to reassemble the shards.

But even now, the world of brokenness we inhabit resides in the bosom of the world of unity, just as each day resides within the larger ocean of memory. God is not yet *one* with God's Name. The prophet Zechariah (14:9) said it: "On that day the Lord will be One and the Name will be One." So now, the closest Jews come to having a creed reads:

SHEMA: Pay attention,

YISROAEL: You who struggle with God.

ADONAI: Being in all its variegated forms is

ELOHAYNU: Our God and

ADONAI: All being is

EHAD: One,

YEHIDO SHEL OLAM: The Only One of Being.

In my youth, Reform Judaism translated the Shema, "Hear, O Israel, the Lord our God, the Lord is One."

We were taught that Judaism deserves great merit for being the first monotheism. This raises, on reflection, two questions: (1) Was Judaism really the first monotheistic religion? (2) Is this worthy of applause?

The first answer, to one neither a historian nor a zealot, must be open to argument. Different experts will hold differing views, and there is always the possibility of new historical information.

As to the second, we Reform Jews of that day were, I believe, presented with a tautology: Jews are worthy of praise because we worship, and were the first to worship, one god, which operation is more praiseworthy than polytheism because we Jews say so.

One must consider possible Jewish ethnocentrism. And, perhaps another question presents itself: Are Jews, in fact, monotheistic?

I believe one could argue the contrary.

Just as Christianity elaborates God into three entities, and, further, into saints; just as Buddhism speaks of the differing aspects of the Buddha, we Jews (at least exegetically) choose between the different names of God, and the differing qualities of each name. We have God and the Shehina—*MaMakoma* (the Place), and *MaMakor* (the Source), *MaRahaman* (the merciful), and so on.

It is the nature of any organism (and observance must be classed as such) to expand and elaborate.

We differentiate further between the *non*-Biblical cognomens of God (*HaMakom, HaMakor, HaRahaman*), and the distinct "powers" of each name and attribute. And, of course, we have the conundrum of the plural, *Elohim*.

It is human nature to create a cosmogony (it is no accident that there are twelve tribes of Israel and twelve major Roman deities, and twelve months of the year—what is Jacob's labored arithmetic in the matter of Ephraim and Manasseh other than the desire to maintain the constant number?). Perhaps our self-awarded satisfaction at the pedigrees of our monotheism is both specious and unnecessary.

To me, the Shema, the profession of Jewish faith is not that God is One, but, putting the verb earlier, that Adonai is our God, that Adonai—whatever god's nature may be—is, finally, beyond knowing, beyond male or female, beyond the artificial construct "single or multiple," beyond our power to denominate—not that God is one, but that God is *whole*.

הִשָּׁמֶר לְךָ פֶּן־תִּשְׁכַּח אֶת־יְדֹוָד אֱלֹהֶיךָ לְבִלְתִּי שְׁמֹר
מִצְוֹתָיו וּמִשְׁפָּטָיו וְחֻקֹּתָיו אֲשֶׁר אָנֹכִי מְצַוְּךָ הַיּוֹם:
פֶּן־תֹּאכַל וְשָׂבָעְתָּ וּבָתִּים טֹבִים תִּבְנֶה וְיָשָׁבְתָּ: וּבְקָרְךָ
וְצֹאנְךָ יִרְבְּיֻן וְכֶסֶף וְזָהָב יִרְבֶּה־לָּךְ וְכֹל אֲשֶׁר־לְךָ
יִרְבֶּה: וְרָם לְבָבֶךָ וְשָׁכַחְתָּ אֶת־יְדֹוָד אֱלֹהֶיךָ הַמּוֹצִיאֲךָ
מֵאֶרֶץ מִצְרַיִם מִבֵּית עֲבָדִים: הַמּוֹלִיכֲךָ בַּמִּדְבָּר הַגָּדֹל
וְהַנּוֹרָא נָחָשׁ שָׂרָף וְעַקְרָב וְצִמָּאוֹן אֲשֶׁר אֵין־מָיִם
הַמּוֹצִיא לְךָ מַיִם מִצּוּר הַחַלָּמִישׁ: הַמַּאֲכִלְךָ מָן
בַּמִּדְבָּר אֲשֶׁר לֹא־יָדְעוּן אֲבֹתֶיךָ לְמַעַן עַנֹּתְךָ וּלְמַעַן
נַסֹּתֶךָ לְהֵיטִבְךָ בְּאַחֲרִיתֶךָ: וְאָמַרְתָּ בִּלְבָבֶךָ כֹּחִי וְעֹצֶם
יָדִי עָשָׂה לִי אֶת־הַחַיִל הַזֶּה: וְזָכַרְתָּ אֶת־יְדֹוָד אֱלֹהֶיךָ
כִּי הוּא הַנֹּתֵן לְךָ כֹּחַ לַעֲשׂוֹת חָיִל לְמַעַן הָקִים
אֶת־בְּרִיתוֹ אֲשֶׁר־נִשְׁבַּע לַאֲבֹתֶיךָ כַּיּוֹם הַזֶּה:

A nd you become arrogant and forget the Lord
your God—who brought you out of the land
of Egypt, the house of bondage, who led you
through the great and terrible wilderness of poisonous
snakes and scorpions and thirst, where there was no water,
who brought you water from the flint rock, who fed you in
the wilderness with manna which your fathers had not

known, in order to make you humble, in order to temper you, in order to ultimately make it good. And you say to yourselves, "My own strength and the power of my own hand have attained this wealth for me." Remember that it is the Lord our God who gives you the power to attain wealth, in order to fulfill the covenant that God promised to make with your parents as it is now.

LK

You get cocky, you start to think that you are running the show, that you are autonomous, have pulled off a few things, that you are in charge, in business for yourself. You are even so shrewd, clever, charmed, and powerful that you can not only beat the odds but make them any way you like. Sure, someday you'll die but not until a ripe old age and then in your sleep. Surely someone that special can even be permitted an occasional moral lapse without guilt or punishment.

"The foundation and the root of estrangement from God and the source of all sins," taught Tzadok HaKohen of Lublin (d. 1900), "comes from saying that God does not supervise creation and that everything is only happenstance, without reckoning, without purpose."

In Deuteronomy, as almost always, the idea is set in terms of retribution, guilt, punishment, and covenant. But it is the same idea: Everything comes from God. What is the alternative? That only some things come from God? But then from where do the *other* things come? The devil? Happenstance? Another God? Ourselves? No, our freedom from the stifling servitude of Egypt and all her fetish-gods was only so that we might now realize and acknowledge a new One of all being, a One who is the source of everything.

Who was it who found water where there was no water, love where there was no love, forgiveness and peace where it did not exist—not where it was insusceptible to our reason, or to our perception, but *where it was not?*

Put differently "who is beyond and different from this human necessity to unify—who took us into the sea on dry land?" Reason is not the ultimate good, but merely a species-specific survival mechanism, and, like any human mechanism, subject to misuse, corruption, and decay.

כִּי יְסִיתְךָ אָחִיךָ בֶן־אִמֶּךָ אוֹ־בִנְךָ אוֹ־בִתְּךָ אוֹ אֵשֶׁת
חֵיקֶךָ אוֹ רֵעֲךָ אֲשֶׁר כְּנַפְשְׁךָ בַּסֵּתֶר לֵאמֹר נֵלְכָה
וְנַעַבְדָה אֱלֹקִים   אֲחֵרִים אֲשֶׁר לֹא יָדַעְתָּ אַתָּה
וַאֲבֹתֶיךָ: מֵאֱלֹהֵי הָעַמִּים אֲשֶׁר סְבִיבֹתֵיכֶם הַקְּרֹבִים
אֵלֶיךָ אוֹ הָרְחֹקִים מִמֶּךָּ מִקְצֵה הָאָרֶץ וְעַד־קְצֵה
הָאָרֶץ: לֹא־תֹאבֶה לוֹ וְלֹא תִשְׁמַע אֵלָיו וְלֹא־תָחוֹס
עֵינְךָ עָלָיו וְלֹא־תַחְמֹל וְלֹא־תְכַסֶּה עָלָיו: כִּי הָרֹג
תַּהַרְגֶנּוּ יָדְךָ תִּהְיֶה־בּוֹ בָרִאשׁוֹנָה לַהֲמִיתוֹ וְיַד כָּל־הָעָם
בָּאַחֲרֹנָה:

I
f your brother—your mother's son—or your son or
your daughter, or the wife of your bosom, or your best
friend entices you in secret, saying, "Come, let us worship other gods"—whom neither you nor your parents
have known—from among the gods of the peoples around
you, either nearby you or far away from you—from one
end of the earth to the other: Do not listen nor pay any attention to him. Show him no pity nor compassion, do not
shield him. You shall kill him; let your hand be the first
upon him to put him to death and later will come the hand
of all the people.

Why, of all the proscriptions against all the horrible things human beings can do to one another, does the Torah have zero tolerance for this one? This worshipping other gods must be especially heinous. There is only one possible explanation for the harshness of this punishment: Everyone must be doing it.

What could possibly lead someone to serve a god unknown to him and his parents? He disdains both himself and his history. He secretly fears that he is worthless and that all his stories are worthless. He even imagines that what he has heard from his own parents has no value. And, even worse, he has come to suspect that if he switches, he will find self-respect at last.

And what could possibly lead someone to seduce someone else into such self-rejection? Fearing his own mistake, he now mollifies his regret by persuading his best friend to commit the same error.

But why capital punishment? Because it is of literally vital importance that there be something holy at the core of a society. There's one thing you just don't screw around with: God is God. And no one else.

DM

A psychoanalytic inversion of this might suggest that the wife, son, or brother, in saying "Let us investigate other gods," *is destroying him- or herself*. That they have sacrificed serenity for intellectuality, and integrity for a supposed "power to choose" which demagoguery we see used to oppress many an individual, populace, or electorate in the name of "freedom."

כִּי־תָבֹא אֶל־הָאָרֶץ אֲשֶׁר יְהוָֹה אֱלֹהֶיךָ נֹתֵן לָךְ
וִירִשְׁתָּהּ וְיָשַׁבְתָּה בָּהּ וְאָמַרְתָּ אָשִׂימָה עָלַי מֶלֶךְ
כְּכָל־הַגּוֹיִם אֲשֶׁר סְבִיבֹתָי: שׂוֹם תָּשִׂים עָלֶיךָ מֶלֶךְ
אֲשֶׁר יִבְחַר יְהוָֹה אֱלֹהֶיךָ בּוֹ מִקֶּרֶב אַחֶיךָ תָּשִׂים עָלֶיךָ
מֶלֶךְ לֹא תוּכַל לָתֵת עָלֶיךָ אִישׁ נָכְרִי אֲשֶׁר לֹא־אָחִיךָ
הוּא: רַק לֹא־יַרְבֶּה־לּוֹ סוּסִים וְלֹא־יָשִׁיב אֶת־הָעָם
מִצְרַיְמָה לְמַעַן הַרְבּוֹת סוּס וַיהוָֹה אָמַר לָכֶם לֹא
תֹסִפוּן לָשׁוּב בַּדֶּרֶךְ הַזֶּה עוֹד: וְלֹא יַרְבֶּה־לּוֹ נָשִׁים
וְלֹא יָסוּר לְבָבוֹ וְכֶסֶף וְזָהָב לֹא יַרְבֶּה־לּוֹ מְאֹד:

Whenyou come into the land that the
Lord your God is giving you, and you
take possession of it and settle in it and
you say, "I will set over myself a king, like all the
nations round about me," you may indeed set a king
over yourself, whom the Lord your God will select. Be
sure to designate as king over your someone from the
midst of your own people; you must not designate a foreigner over you, someone who is not your kinsman. Furthermore, he shall not keep many horses or take the
people back to Egypt to increase the number of his horses, since God has said to you, "You must not go back

that way again." And he shall not have many wives, lest his heart go astray; nor shall he amass silver and gold to excess.

W hy on earth would you have to *tell* a people *not* to choose a foreigner for their king? No Egyptian complained when Pharaoh made Joseph king of Egypt, nor did a Persian when Ahasuerus picked Mordecai to rule over Persia. And both of them did fine jobs.

Is it simply a fear of political assimilation? (And if it is, then what shall we do with Zionism's principal argument that the Jews need their own state *just like everybody else.*)

Or is it a projection back into the wilderness past of some hard-learned wisdom of disillusionment with kings and their avarice. Hadn't the prophet Samuel also admonished Israel against this very error? Certainly by the time Judea and Israel split apart, King Solomon had amassed silver and gold, horses, and no less than six hundred wives. And Solomon was an Israelite!

Perhaps, as we see elsewhere in the Hebrew Bible, it is a divine concession to human weakness. "I was hoping to be your king," laments God. "But if you insist on a king of flesh and blood, then at least don't let him act like one!" The utopian nation with God as king cannot work because of human nature, just as an ordinary one with a mortal as its king doesn't work because of human nature either! A native on the throne might occasionally seek divine guidance. That's Israel for you.

DM

A Jew wrote, "Man is born free, yet everywhere he is in chains."

It was foreseen that Israel would request a king. This is perhaps a reiteration of the story of Babel—enough people in one place will, sooner or later, elaborate individual interactions into an organization and the organization will inevitably create a hierarchy. Any organization exists primarily to ensure its own continuation—it must elaborate a way of finding, by Darwinian means, the best strategy for survival. Judaism survives—if not "intact," then, say, recognizably, as devotion to study. Historically, oppression and lack of statehood have curtailed organizational elaboration.

The acknowledgment that "you shall surely set over yourselves a king" is followed by a resigned and less than hopeful litany of protective or countervailing suggestions—let him not have too much gold, too many horses, too many wives—and it is bracketed by sad, resigned references to the inevitable consequences of humanity—the story of Babel. Do not erect for yourselves a pillar (16:22), and Egyptian slavery, "He shall not multiply horses to himself, and cause the people to return toward Egypt." (17:16).

The king's desire for horses will return the people to Egypt; our desire for a king, a human embodiment of the divine, will, and does, return us *Mitzrayimah*—toward Egypt.

זָכוֹר אֵת אֲשֶׁר־עָשָׂה לְךָ עֲמָלֵק בַּדֶּרֶךְ בְּצֵאתְכֶם
מִמִּצְרָיִם: אֲשֶׁר קָרְךָ בַּדֶּרֶךְ וַיְזַנֵּב בְּךָ כָּל־הַנֶּחֱשָׁלִים
אַחֲרֶיךָ וְאַתָּה עָיֵף וְיָגֵעַ וְלֹא יָרֵא אֱלֹקִים: וְהָיָה בְּהָנִיחַ
יְדֹוָד אֱלֹקֶיךָ לְךָ מִכָּל־אֹיְבֶיךָ מִסָּבִיב בָּאָרֶץ אֲשֶׁר
יְדֹוָד־אֱלֹקֶיךָ נֹתֵן לְךָ נַחֲלָה לְרִשְׁתָּהּ תִּמְחֶה אֶת־זֵכֶר
עֲמָלֵק מִתַּחַת הַשָּׁמָיִם לֹא תִּשְׁכָּח:

emember what Amalek did to you on the way
when you went out of Egypt: how, when you
were tired and weary, he did not fear of God and
he fell upon you on the way and cut down all the strag-
glers in your rear. Therefore, when the Lord your God
grants you safety from all your enemies round about you
in the land that the Lord your God is giving you as a
hereditary portion, you shall blot out the memory of
Amalek from under heaven. Do not forget!

Rabbi Zalman Schachter-Shalomi is fond of reminding us that after the play, the villain comes out and usually gets the biggest applause of all. This means, I suspect, that Pharaoh and Haman, and, yes, even Amalek, work for God. Our sages teach, in *Midrash Mishlei* 9:2, that when the Messiah comes, all the holidays will be abrogated except for Purim. If the idea of Haman (the paradigm enemy of the Jews, who himself is descended from Amalek) is abrogated, then it means that there are no villains, and that is only another way of saying that the bad guys are not all that bad and the good guys are not all that good. A man I know who once kept getting into fights with one of his coworkers was asked by his supervisor to visit the company psychologist. "When I sat down in his office, the psychologist looked at me and asked, 'What is there about your coworker that reminds you of yourself?' " My friend said, "I thanked the therapist, left his office, and never had a problem with my coworker again."

We must remember what Amalek did, and we are commanded to wipe out Amalek's memory. How do we expunge the memory? *Only* through memory. Repression inevitably increases and prolongs trauma as the individual (or race) deals with both the original assault and the additional and loathsome burden of its constant, hypocritical reinterpretation.

וְעָנִיתָ וְאָמַרְתָּ לִפְנֵי יְדֹוָד אֱלֹקֶיךָ אֲרַמִּי אֹבֵד אָבִי וַיֵּרֶד
מִצְרַיְמָה וַיָּגָר שָׁם בִּמְתֵי מְעָט וַיְהִי־שָׁם לְגוֹי גָּדוֹל
עָצוּם וָרָב: וַיָּרֵעוּ אֹתָנוּ הַמִּצְרִים וַיְעַנּוּנוּ וַיִּתְּנוּ עָלֵינוּ
עֲבֹדָה קָשָׁה: וַנִּצְעַק אֶל־יְדֹוָד אֱלֹקֵי אֲבֹתֵינוּ וַיִּשְׁמַע
יְדֹוָד אֶת־קֹלֵנוּ וַיַּרְא אֶת־עָנְיֵנוּ וְאֶת־עֲמָלֵנוּ
וְאֶת־לַחֲצֵנוּ: וַיּוֹצִאֵנוּ יְדֹוָד מִמִּצְרַיִם בְּיָד חֲזָקָה וּבִזְרֹעַ
נְטוּיָה וּבְמֹרָא גָּדֹל וּבְאֹתוֹת וּבְמֹפְתִים: וַיְבִאֵנוּ
אֶל־הַמָּקוֹם הַזֶּה וַיִּתֶּן־לָנוּ אֶת־הָאָרֶץ הַזֹּאת אֶרֶץ זָבַת
חָלָב וּדְבָשׁ: וְעַתָּה הִנֵּה הֵבֵאתִי אֶת־רֵאשִׁית פְּרִי
הָאֲדָמָה אֲשֶׁר־נָתַתָּה לִּי יְדֹוָד וְהִנַּחְתּוֹ לִפְנֵי יְדֹוָד
אֱלֹקֶיךָ וְהִשְׁתַּחֲוִיתָ לִפְנֵי יְדֹוָד אֱלֹקֶיךָ:

Y ou shall answer and say before the Lord your
God: "My father was a wandering Aramean.
He went down to Egypt few in number and
sojourned there; but there he became a great and very pop-
ulous nation. The Egyptians dealt harshly with us and
oppressed us; they imposed heavy labor upon us. We cried
out to the Lord, the God of our parents, and God heard our
cry and saw our affliction, our misery, and our oppression. And God brought us out from Egypt with a mighty

hand and an outstretched arm and with awesome power, and by signs and wonders. God brought us to this place and gave us this land, a land flowing with milk and honey. Therefore I now bring the first fruits of the soil which You, O God, have given me."

Of all the passages tradition could select as the literary core of the Haggadah—the narratives and poetry of Exodus, the plagues, the watch night, the going out from slavery, the splitting of the sea, the song at the sea—why choose this obscure recitation meant to accompany the lost ritual of bringing the first fruits to the local priest? And then, why truncate the passage before the last verse about how God brought us to this land flowing with milk and honey, omitting it from the Haggadah's discussion?

Could it be the vestige of a time when the spring festival of freedom was initially the celebration of the first fruits of the barley harvest (now baked into unleavened cakes of bread) and the birth of the first lamb of the flock (now only a shank bone on the seder plate), the memory of a time when our gratitude was expressed tangibly. "Here, God. Who am I kidding? There's no way I could have done this by myself. The first yield of my labors and prayer belong to You." But we, born into freedom, have ourselves yet to make the offer of such similarly precious gifts to God. So at best we can only rehearse the words and deeds of our foreparents. We are not yet permitted to expostulate and fantasize about what it would be like to live in a land flowing with milk and honey, which, as the psychologist David Bakan once suggested, was baby food.

DM

We testify before the priest not only that we cried out and we were heard, but that our own actions led to our afflictions—we went *down* to Egypt and were ill treated and oppressed.

Were we oppressed there because we became numerous, or in spite of our numbers, or because we went down to Egypt?

Was there an error in the wandering Aramean, the Aramean who was "passing through"—going down toward Egypt—or was the error in his sojourning there, or in his descendants accepting as permanent a situation he intended only to be temporary? Or was there no error at all? Just an inconclusive, endlessly provocative history?

כִּי הַמִּצְוָה הַזֹּאת אֲשֶׁר אָנֹכִי מְצַוְּךָ הַיּוֹם לֹא־נִפְלֵאת
הִוא מִמְּךָ וְלֹא־רְחֹקָה הִוא: לֹא בַשָּׁמַיִם הִוא לֵאמֹר
מִי יַעֲלֶה־לָּנוּ הַשָּׁמַיְמָה וְיִקָּחֶהָ לָּנוּ וְיַשְׁמִעֵנוּ אֹתָהּ
וְנַעֲשֶׂנָּה: וְלֹא־מֵעֵבֶר לַיָּם הִוא לֵאמֹר מִי יַעֲבָר־לָנוּ
אֶל־עֵבֶר הַיָּם וְיִקָּחֶהָ לָּנוּ וְיַשְׁמִעֵנוּ אֹתָהּ וְנַעֲשֶׂנָּה:
כִּי־קָרוֹב אֵלֶיךָ הַדָּבָר מְאֹד בְּפִיךָ וּבִלְבָבְךָ לַעֲשֹׂתוֹ:

Surely, this commandment which I command you this day is not too awesome for you, nor is it beyond reach. It is not in the heavens that you should say, "Who among us can go up to the heavens and take it for us and cause us to hear it so that we may do it?" Neither is it across the sea that you should say, "Who among us can cross over the sea and take it for us and cause us to hear it so that we may do it." No, the thing is very close to you, already in your mouth and in your heart, to do it.

o, the Torah is not somewhere else. It's already in us. We're made of it. It is to our consciousness like the double helix coil of deoxyribonucleic acid is to our bodies. Torah is, in other words, already coded into our very protoplasm. And that's why it feels so good to live by the Torah (The Way of All Being); we're just doing what we've been designed for from the very beginning.

Some commentators, noting that the Hebrew does not say "instruction" but "commandment," wisely suggest that the "commandment" here that is already in our mouths and hearts is "teshuva, returning to God." This may indeed just be the mother of all the commandments, the only thing God really says, all the other commandments being only human refractions and imaginings of the one "word." All God ever says is "Return to Me." You don't need to go anywhere. You're already there. You can hear it everywhere: in the wind and the rustling of the leaves; in the clink of money in a beggar's cup, the coo of lovers, and the cry of those in pain; it's in the moisture on your tongue, the effortless emptying and filling of your lungs, and the rhythm throb of your pulse—"Return to Me."

What is it that Moses receives up on Mount Sinai? Only the permission to hear what has already been within him and the rest of us all along, the one utterance which may ultimately be the same as Torah: "Return to Me."

DM

We are not a religion of intercessors, saints, and hierarchies of gods.

There is nothing between us and the Deity.

The Torah exists, and we as Jews are not only free, not only encouraged, but constitutionally disposed, to debate it and interpret it. Yet we are told that there was no one like Moses, and there never will be again. His election can only be borne—his glory and intimacy with God will not be repeated. And we need not aspire to that post—the position has been filled. We don't have to like this idea, but we do have to live with it. The mitigation is this: That we are never to be subjected to such again—each Jew since Moses has an absolutely equal share in the Torah and the word of God. "It is not in Heaven, where we must send someone" to hear it for us. It is in our mouth, and in our hand."

Eugene Debs, the great socialist activist and philosopher said: "Even if I could, I would not lead you into the Promised Land. For if I could lead you in, someone else could lead you out."

וַיְדַבֵּר יְהֹוָה אֶל־מֹשֶׁה בְּעֶצֶם הַיּוֹם הַזֶּה לֵאמֹר: עֲלֵה
אֶל־הַר הָעֲבָרִים הַזֶּה הַר־נְבוֹ אֲשֶׁר בְּאֶרֶץ מוֹאָב
אֲשֶׁר עַל־פְּנֵי יְרֵחוֹ וּרְאֵה אֶת־אֶרֶץ כְּנַעַן אֲשֶׁר אֲנִי
נֹתֵן לִבְנֵי יִשְׂרָאֵל לַאֲחֻזָּה: וּמֻת בָּהָר אֲשֶׁר אַתָּה עֹלֶה
שָׁמָּה וְהֵאָסֵף אֶל־עַמֶּיךָ כַּאֲשֶׁר־מֵת אַהֲרֹן אָחִיךָ בְּהֹר
הָהָר וַיֵּאָסֶף אֶל־עַמָּיו: עַל אֲשֶׁר מְעַלְתֶּם בִּי בְּתוֹךְ בְּנֵי
יִשְׂרָאֵל בְּמֵי־מְרִיבַת קָדֵשׁ מִדְבַּר־צִן עַל אֲשֶׁר
לֹא־קִדַּשְׁתֶּם אוֹתִי בְּתוֹךְ בְּנֵי יִשְׂרָאֵל: כִּי מִנֶּגֶד תִּרְאֶה
אֶת־הָאָרֶץ וְשָׁמָּה לֹא תָבוֹא אֶל־הָאָרֶץ אֲשֶׁר־אֲנִי נֹתֵן
לִבְנֵי יִשְׂרָאֵל:

And God spoke to Moses this very day saying:
"Ascend these heights of Abarim to Mount
Nebo, which is in the land of Moab facing
Jericho, and view the land of Canaan, which I am giving the children of Israel as their possession. You shall
die on the mountain that you are about to ascend, and
shall be gathered to your kin, as your brother Aaron
died on Mount Hor and was gathered to his kin; because
you both rose up against Me among the children of Is-

rael, at the waters of Meribah-Kadesh in the wilderness of Zin; you did not sanctify Me among the children of Israel. From a distance you may view the land—the land I am giving to the children of Israel, but into it you shall not go.

It has always struck me as a lousy deal that, after all they'd been through together, God wouldn't let Moses enter the Promised Land. Sure, he hit the rock twice and smote the Egyptian, but everything in the last four books has been about Moses leading the Israelites to cross the Jordan. What harm could it do? In some of the most heartrending *midrashim*, Moses begs for just a few more days of life. And, when even that is denied, he pleads simply to be a bird that could fly *over* the land and at least view it from the sky. Again, God says no.

But it wasn't until I indulged my fantasy that I understood what Moses and we are being taught. What if God had acceded to Moses' request?

"Okay, Moses, you win. I give you permission to enter the land."

"Oh, thank you, Lord," replies Moses. "For a man one hundred twenty years old, to splash through the Jordan, this is indeed a great gift. Say, I was wondering too, God, if you might also let me visit Majorca before I die. I hear that it's supposed to be beautiful this time of year."

And then I understood. God understands all our humanity and says to Moses (and us, if we want): "Moses, My faithful shepherd, I will bestow on you something even more wonderful than visiting yet another new land. I will take you up on this mountain and let you see with new eyes."

DM

The Torah is fitted to our understanding.

Moses is told that he may not enter the Promised Land because of what would seem a trifling incident at the well of Meribah.

But may we not see his exclusion as a blessing?

He was, we are told, a faithful servant. How wonderful for him, then, to be given his rest in sight of his goal, but spared from the quotidian, enervating, anguishing results attendant upon his work's completion.

Any triumph, any absolute end must be followed by a period of emptiness, loss, dejection, and self-doubt.

If we live long enough past any achievement we can see, in retrospect, our pride in it as vanity, our enjoyment of its blessings (for ourselves and others) eroded by their attendant misuse. We are left with the choice either of cynicism or dedication to a new goal.

But we view this new goal now not innocently, but with the burden of fatigue, disillusionment, perhaps with a sense of entitlement feeling; perhaps, that one so accomplished should, in the course of

events, be spared the necessity of a return to frightened humility.

But we cannot cease.

The self-doubt, the drive for understanding, which
are part of the human condition and are certainly the
state of the Jew, impel us to begin again.

Had God informed Moses, "You have performed
perfectly, now enter and receive your reward," Moses
would have had no reward at all. He was left to assess
for himself his accomplishments, to find them not
without merit, but imperfect. He was given from on
high that humility which alone permits us to begin
the new thing, and was thus released.

וְלֹא־קָם נָבִיא עוֹד בְּיִשְׂרָאֵל כְּמֹשֶׁה אֲשֶׁר יְדָעוֹ יְדֹוָד
פָּנִים אֶל־פָּנִים: לְכָל־הָאֹתֹת וְהַמּוֹפְתִים אֲשֶׁר שְׁלָחוֹ
יְדֹוָד   לַעֲשׂוֹת בְּאֶרֶץ מִצְרַיִם לְפַרְעֹה וּלְכָל־עֲבָדָיו
וּלְכָל־אַרְצוֹ: וּלְכֹל הַיָּד הַחֲזָקָה וּלְכֹל הַמּוֹרָא הַגָּדוֹל
אֲשֶׁר עָשָׂה מֹשֶׁה לְעֵינֵי כָּל־יִשְׂרָאֵל:

Never again has there arisen in Israel a prophet like Moses—whom God knew, face-to-face, for the various signs and wonders that God sent him to perform in the land of Egypt, against Pharaoh and all his courtiers and his whole country, and for all the great might and awesome power that Moses displayed before all Israel.

LK

As important as Moses certainly is, Jewish tradition, probably fearing his deification, keeps him at arm's length. The sins which kept him out of the Promised Land are routinely rehearsed, we are constantly reminded of his role as conduit for the divine voice rather than religious innovator, and his name is not even mentioned in the Passover Haggadah. Yes, he was the greatest of all prophets and blessed with a clearer vision of God than any other human being, but Moses died like everyone else. He didn't even make it across the Jordan. And the Haftarah, the liturgical portion selected from the prophetic books to be read in conjunction with this final lection, comes from the first chapter of the next book, Joshua. Here we learn that it is for Moses' disciple, Moses' student, to lead the children of Israel into the Promised Land.

DM

Any organism exists primarily to perpetuate itself. As it grows, it accrues substance, and its vigor attracts both acolytes and parasites; their voracity for life, in turn, will help turn the balance from growth and toward the inevitable decay which is the lot of the organic.

Disraeli, a Jew, called Christianity, "completed Judaism." But Judaism cannot be "completed" beyond the Torah and live. The Torah may be interpreted and reinterpreted but it cannot be completed.

The Torah ends with a most forceful and final injunction to remember that Moses' like shall not be seen again, that never again will there be an intermediary, that no human will stand face-to-face with God.

The "struggle with the angel," Judaism's struggle, is this: not that we will wrest more information from him—we will not—but that we learn to live with the information we possess—to cease seeking information and to pursue wisdom.

ABOUT THE AUTHORS

LAWRENCE KUSHNER teaches and writes as The Emanu-El Scholar at The Congregation Emanu-El of San Francisco. He has taught at Hebrew Union College-Jewish Institute of Religion in New York City and served for twenty-eight years as rabbi of Congregation Beth El in Sudbury, Massachusetts. A frequent lecturer, he is also the author of more than a dozen books on Jewish spirituality and mysticism. He lives in San Francisco.

DAVID MAMET is a Pulitzer Prize–winning playwright. He is the author of *Glengarry Glen Ross*, *The Cryptogram*, *American Buffalo*, and *Boston Marriage*, among other plays. He has also published three novels and many screenplays, children's books, and collections of essays.